∞

Transforming Your Life
Through the Eucharist

Also available from
Sophia Institute Press®
by John A. Kane:

Conquering Your Sins
With Heartfelt Repentance

The School of Mary

Six Lessons for Life
from the School of the Cross

John A. Kane

Transforming
Your Life
Through the
Eucharist

SOPHIA INSTITUTE PRESS®
Manchester, New Hampshire

Transforming Your Life Through the Eucharist was originally published in 1941 by St. Anthony Guild Press, New Jersey, under the title *The School of Love*. This 1999 edition by Sophia Institute Press contains minor editorial revisions to the original text.

Sophia Institute Press®
Box 5284, Manchester, NH 03108
1-800-888-9344
www.sophiainstitute.com

Nihil Obstat: Henry Zolzer, *Censor librorum*
Imprimatur: Thomas H. McLaughlin, Bishop of Paterson, Feast of Corpus Christi, 1941

Library of Congress Cataloging-in-Publication Data

Kane, John A., 1883-
    [School of love]
    Transforming your life through the Eucharist / John A. Kane.
       p.   cm.
    Originally published: School of love. Paterson, N. J. : St. Anthony
    Guild Press, 1941.
    Includes bibliographical references.
    ISBN 0-918477-90-5 (alk. paper)
    1. Lord's Supper — Catholic Church. 2. Catholic Church
    Prayerbooks and devotions — English. I. Title
BX2169.K35 1999
234'.163 — dc21   98-54343 CIP

99 00 01 02 03   10 9 8 7 6 5 4 3 2

Contents

∞

Transforming Your Life
Through the Eucharist

Editor's Note: The biblical references in the following pages are based on the Douay-Rheims edition of the Old and New Testaments. Where applicable, biblical quotations have been cross-referenced with the differing names and enumeration in the Revised Standard Version, using the following symbol: (RSV =).

Chapter One

∽

You can become
one with Christ

Daily "from the rising of the sun unto the going down of the same,"[1] the marvelous act of Consecration, first performed by Christ in the Cenacle,[2] is perpetuated by His chosen priesthood on every Catholic altar. The same God who then gave Himself so unreservedly to the favored Twelve, now gives Himself really, truly, and substantially to you and to me. The same eternally efficacious Sacrifice is daily offered up among us as the gift of the Son of God. The eucharistic oblation is not only a memorial, but is also a constant renewal, a prolongation, a continual manifestation, of the transcendent act of Christ by the same God of almighty power whose "delights were to be with the children of men."[3]

Corpus Christi, the festival in which the Church annually commemorates the institution of the Holy Eucharist, logically follows the other festivals of the Incarnation because it is the complete fulfillment of their sublime purpose, their glorious end. Christ's birth, death, Resurrection, and Ascension, and the coming of the Holy Spirit — each glitters as a golden link

---

[1] Ps. 112:3 (RSV = Ps. 113:3).

[2] From the Latin *cenaculum*, or "eating room," often located in the upper story of a house. The Cenacle is where the Last Supper took place.

[3] Prov. 8:31.

in that wondrous chain of ineffable mercies uniting earth with Heaven; the one eternal reason for them all was His infinite yearning to reign in souls. "My delights are to be with the children of men." His sacramental Presence effects this union.

The Holy Eucharist is, then, the flower of the Incarnation, the completion of all the mysteries of the Redeemer's life as Man. The institution of the Blessed Sacrament was the consummation of the stupendous series of God's merciful dispensations to His fallen creatures, for Christ came "to seek and to save that which was lost"[4] by giving Himself to man. The end of His Passion, death, and glorification in our nature was that He might forever dwell in His Mystical Body, and therefore in us, members of that Mystical Body, the Church.

In this mystery of love inexpressible, Christ unites Himself with us. The purpose of every act of His earthly life was the realization of the most intimate union with man. The Holy Eucharist seals and perpetuates this closest of unions. Hence divine love, the most striking of God's manifestations, stands alone in this august Sacrament, because it is the soul of this mystery.

In the Holy Eucharist, divine love restrains omnipotence; infinite justice ceases to urge its inexorable claims on sinners. In this mystery, the infinite God is bound by space; the Eternal God is conditioned by time; the divine immensity descends to our littleness; the light of God's unspeakable beauty and majestic glory, which floods Heaven, filling the saints with rapturous delight, conceals its radiant splendor before our weak eyes, and adapts itself to the dimness of our sight, which can

[4] Luke 19:10.

behold the unseen only "through a glass in a dark manner."[5] In this mystery, no sacrifice is too great, because every attribute of the infinite Lover of men yields to His intense longing to be one with souls, to thrill them with ecstatic joy, "to inebriate them with the plenty of His house,"[6] to lavish upon them His divinity by a condescension so immeasurable, and a humiliation so profound, as to elude the grasp of the keenest of even angelic minds.

Furthermore, Christ's manifestation of Himself in the Blessed Sacrament is entirely new and absolutely different from any other revelation of Himself to the creature. The wail for forty centuries, begun at the gate of Eden, of man's sorely afflicted soul — "O give me back my God!" — was his heart's cry for immediate surcease of sorrow, for light at once to dispel his darkness, for spiritual food quickly to appease his famished soul. This was, however, but the faint expression of the most vehement yearning of his being for the munificent gift of Heaven. The Holy Eucharist is the answer to man's burning desire for his God.

What wonder, then, that we feel in our moral lives effects so signal after Holy Communion, an overflow of indefinable joy, a consuming heavenly sweetness, an almost miraculous transformation, an exulting consciousness of a new life rising up within us and pervading our souls. A yet greater wonder is the presence of the eucharistic God in us in a nature glorified, but nevertheless like our own, for He assumed our flesh. If recollected, we feel keenly the presence of the sacramental Savior!

[5] 1 Cor. 13:12.
[6] Cf. Ps. 35:9 (RSV = Ps. 36:8).

We are united with Christ, incomparably closer than heat with fire, closer than color with its object. Only omnipotence could establish a union so intimate, so perfect, so wonderful.

O incomprehensible mystery, masterpiece of infinite wisdom, boundless goodness, almighty power, eternal love! The creature, the helpless child of dust, receives and assimilates the Eternal God! The God of whose immensity we have but a hazy notion, dwells in the closest of unions with man! Divine love, eternally constant, blends with human love; so ephemeral, so inconstant that it cannot count on its own steadfastness one instant!

What a vista of sublime thought this mystery unfolds to the reflective mind! How it visualizes the sanctity that should adorn the soul once the eucharistic King enters into it! He becomes one with us to supernaturalize every faculty, every thought, every desire, every sense, and every act. He strives to rivet our attention on Heaven; to free us, in our struggle for salvation, from the most abject servitude of our worst enemy; to annihilate unmortified self, that He may wholly preoccupy us, for when He takes possession of us, His mind must be ours.

Self-denial must be the fixed law of our lives. Self must be sublimed; the natural disciplined by the supernatural; the flesh mastered; inordinate love of the world completely stifled; and every power of the soul must assume the tone and character of a life fully dedicated to His service, so that all alone, in the silent solitude of our recollected beings, He may whisper in accents of divine love, "This is my rest. . . . Here will I dwell, for I have chosen it."[7]

---

[7] Ps. 131:14 (Ps. 132:14).

And like the God of the Eucharist, concealed under the humblest of elements, hiddenness must distinguish our lives. We see Christ in the Blessed Sacrament, not with our bodily eyes, but with the highest and most wondrous spiritual vision — pure faith. As the Savior hid the glory and grandeur of the Godhead in His assumption of our nature, so, too, in the Holy Eucharist there is no visible disclosure of Him. Consequently, to be one with Him in loving harmony, we must be hidden with Him;[8] we must be lost in Him. We must die to ourselves that we may live to Him. The criticism of our actions, favorable or adverse, should neither elate nor dispirit us. The sublimity and condescension of our God should deeply concern and wholly absorb us.

In the Catholic sanctuary, all is still. In marked contrast with the feverish excitement of the world without, the dwelling of the eucharistic King is a paradise of blissful repose. From His visible throne among us, He diffuses an eternal stillness that transfixes even the unbeliever. Christ's earthly home is the silent abode of abiding rest, the solemnly silent abode of abiding rest and perennial peace. Our lives must be silent and calm if we are to be conformed to the Divine Solitary of our altars. Amid life's fitful fluctuations, in the din and pressure of the world around us, we must possess our souls in peace, and thus ever commune with the God of peace, so that He may form in us His image.

In the light of these truths, what reasons we have to humble ourselves to the dust, when we consider our spiritual supineness after so many Holy Communions! How strong is the

[8] Col. 3:3.

impulse of self-love within us, and how easily we are lured by its powerful and insidious appeal, after having received the God who we know cannot tolerate a divided heart! What are our protestations of unswerving fidelity to our Lord and Master but a series of broken promises? How often is our self-will, and not the will of the sacramental Savior, the ruling power of our lives!

When He becomes our guest, we promise never to forsake Him. We consecrate ourselves wholly to Him. But oh how often is our self-surrender a matter of mere words! Possessing Him, we are rapt to ecstasy. We resolve, regardless of the wiles of self-love, to imitate Him, our Model, and to follow Him, our King, wheresoever He leads us by the sweet attraction of His grace.

But then a cloud hardly visible unexpectedly looms up and casts its black shadow over us. Perhaps a friend has, under stress of feeling, spoken somewhat harshly to us, and at once we forget the covenant we made with our God. We have been recreant to our pledges of loyalty. The emotional fervor that we mistook for true devotion immediately after Holy Communion has vanished before the light of day has deepened into dusk.

Again, in the strength of the Bread of Angels invigorating our souls, we determine to "mortify, by the Spirit, the deeds of flesh";[9] to forego many of life's innocent pleasures out of love for Him who, "having joy set before Him, endured the Cross, despising the shame";[10] but how strong and assertive is our

[9] Cf. Rom. 8:13.
[10] Heb. 12:2.

complex self-indulgence! What moral weaklings we are, wrestling with our vicious tendencies! How eagerly we compromise, even though the victory may be won with but little effort! What a disparity between our professions of allegiance to the God of the Eucharist and our self-sacrifice, which is their touchstone!

We are lifted above the earth by the peace of God after receiving Holy Communion, and we strive to preserve this most precious gift by a spirit of recollection, but the world soon disquiets us, and amid its distracting cares, the ideal is all too quickly lost in its conflict with the actual. We are willingly carried away by our schemes for material advancement, and the outward aspect, the incessant activity essential to their success, makes a subtle change in our inner life. The bond of union between us and our God is thus weakened almost before we have been fully conscious of it.

Is He not therefore deeply wounded by our want of love? Is He not bitterly disappointed by our infidelity? Is He not sorely distressed by our inconstancy? But He still abides with us, feeding us daily, bearing with our fickleness and our thoughtlessness. He is constant in His love for us despite our fitful changes. He is "the same, yesterday, today, and forever"[11] — ever kind, ever gracious, ever long-suffering, ever merciful.

He knows best all our shortcomings because He is our God, but He cannot abandon us, because He loves us too much. He silently endures our selfishness and disloyalty. He urgently asks us to be honest and sincere with Him. He attracts us by the divine magnetism of His myriad graces. And oh, how insistently

[11] Cf. Heb. 13:8.

He pleads with us to surrender ourselves to Him, that this Sacrament, the masterpiece of divine love and omnipotent power, may finally awaken a response in our souls that shall, by its deep, penitential love, remit the guilt of our coldness, our ingratitude, and our faithlessness!

That He may bear with us still and help us — such should be our prayer before the patient and loving, the long-suffering Prisoner of the altar. We should beseech Him for one particular grace, the crown of His infinite generosity to us: that He kindle to intense ardor the fire of love which He came to cast on earth[12] — the mighty, burning furnace of which is His sacramental Presence among us — so that we may love Him more ardently and follow Him more closely during our exile, until the veil shall be removed, and we shall see Him as He is;[13] now beholding Him dimly and afar off[14] in His eucharistic abasement, but at last gazing upon Him in the fullness of His divine beauty, when we shall become like unto Him in the brilliant light of the glory that will ravish our souls forever.

[12] Luke 12:49.
[13] 1 John 3:2.
[14] Cf. 1 Cor. 13:12.

Chapter Two

∞

How the Eucharist makes you like Christ

❦

Not directly, but through the humanity of Christ, God gave us His perfect life. In Christ dwells the fullness of divinity from which emanates the glory of His eternal life, wholly inaccessible but imparted to us through its accommodation to our littleness, thus enriching us with His divinity according to our finite capacity. The Holy Eucharist, the sun of Christianity, is the source of this life, and consequently the fountainhead of all grace, all virtue.

In this mystery, union with souls is the amazing, consuming yearning of the sacramental Savior. He abides on every altar as the Author and Finisher of our sanctification. We behold Him there no longer bruised and battered for our sins; no longer is there any visible evidence of the untold mental anguish, the agonizing physical pain, or the bitter desolation which He underwent to redeem us. But in the Holy Eucharist, He is the object of man's indifference and neglect. Although He conquered sin by His death and Resurrection, He is still within the range of the sinner's power to insult and outrage Him. As of old, so today, there are "enemies of the Cross of Christ; whose end is destruction; whose god is their belly; and whose glory is in their shame; who mind earthly things."[16]

[16] Phil. 3:18, 19.

Great, then, and urgent is the need of reparation on our part for the pain of which the eucharistic King is the daily silent Victim. Calm and restful though our gratitude may be in our moments of adoration, we must never forget the studied neglect, the worldliness, of His wayward children, but rather strive persistently with all our powers to comfort Him in His sacramental lowliness, while the storm of sin set in motion by the thoughtlessness, if not the malice, of so many, beats Him as ruthlessly and heartlessly as the steel scourge fell upon His virginal flesh and numbered all His bones.[17]

Christ's loving adaptation of Himself to the limitations and weaknesses of His creatures, despite His foreseeing their utter disregard of Him, is an astounding example of mercy. To facilitate our access to Him is the sole reason for this wondrous adaptation. He veils His presence, thus tempering the glory of His divinity, so that we may come to Him with a confidence born of His infinite love for us. Although hidden, He is really, truly, and substantially present with His humanity, with His divinity, undivided and indivisible, with grace unlimited, with power almighty, and with the absolute perfection of all the virtues of the Godhead.

He is not before us piecemeal. Where His omnipotence is, there also is His love, His mercy, and all His other attributes, for, being essentially one, He cannot be divided. Yet, in adapting His infiniteness to our littleness, in accommodating His unlimited perfections to our limited capacity, He does not diminish by a jot or a tittle[18] the fullness of His majesty and glory.

[17] Ps. 21:18 (RSV = Ps. 22:17).
[18] Cf. Matt. 5:18.

We could not receive Him as He is and live.[19] We could not behold and endure the majestic grandeur of His divinity, if He did not in compassion stoop to our frailty and nothingness. He hides the Presence that entrances the celestial choirs so that He may not overpower us.

How telling is the mercy of His loving condescension! In His divine tenderness and affability, He bestows on us as much of His fullness as we are spiritually able to assimilate. With a compassionate restraint, He contracts Himself to our finite souls. He gives Himself to us according to the measure of our powers of spiritual apprehension, and as we, through correspondence with His grace, advance in virtue, He leads us to height beyond height, broadening and deepening our capacities, thus giving us a more comprehensive grasp of His infinite perfections.

Nevertheless, we receive Christ, not partially, but whole and entire. What a transformation would be wrought in us, if we fully corresponded with the designs of His love in giving Himself entirely to us! To what summits of sanctity would we rise, if we overcame our natural inconstancy! What a change would be worked, how energized our souls would be, if we died to ourselves that we might live to Christ within us!

When we receive Him, all that He is and possesses is ours. With St. Paul, we can exclaim, "I live, now not I, but Christ liveth in me. And that I live now in the flesh, I live in the faith of the Son of God, who loved me, and delivered Himself for me."[20] He enters into us with all the infinite sanctity of His divine life, and all the virtues of His perfect human life.

[19] Cf. Exod. 33:20.
[20] Gal. 2:20.

How much, therefore, depends on our preparation! For although we receive Christ fully, He unfolds His life according to the measure of our cooperation. Unlimited are the possibilities of the eucharistic indwelling, but our resultant spiritual development is slow, because the reception of the fullness of grace in Holy Communion demands our full accord with the Savior's eternal yearning to be one with us.

Did we but give ourselves to Him, assuredly our thoughts and desires, our words and actions, would ever reflect the conscious recognition of His presence within us. As we contend against the angels of darkness, as we battle the hosts of Hell, illumined by the light of Christ and strengthened with His strength, we would conquer them, even if they forced us in the struggle to the very gates of Hell. How intimate the companionship, how close the union with, our God! Did we but realize what it is to receive the food of immortality — Christ possessing us, and we possessing Christ — we would be citizens of earth only by necessity, for our conversation would be in Heaven.[21]

But although we are gradually transformed by the eucharistic God, we are not to infer that our nature changes. The change in us is the entrance into our souls of a higher and holier love, raising them by degrees to a loftier spiritual level. As we progress in a life of calm repose, strong faith, ardent love, persevering prayer, singular purity of intention, and constant vigilance, this higher and holier life assumes full stature and perfect proportions.

What, it is natural to ask, should be the influence of such a life on the souls of our brethren? What Christ is to us, *that* we

---

[21] Phil. 3:20.

18

should be to them. He dwells in us as the primal source of sanctity and strength, elevating the nature that He so lovingly associates with Himself. We must therefore diffuse this sanctity and strength in all our human contacts. In imitation of Christ's purpose in us, as He acts and speaks in us, we should communicate with the souls of others.

Under the benign influence of the Divine Presence, the natural should submit to the supernatural, our souls doing their utmost to lead this higher life, to grow more rapidly in this holier love. With our inward and outward activity under the complete control of Christ, love — the principle of His working within us — will be the law of our relations with our fellowmen. Preoccupied with the absolute certainty of Christ's Presence, we will be filled with religious fervor. We will sanctify others, for Christ within us will always ennoble the world around us.

How distressing, then, it is that we human habitations of the eucharistic God speak and act so often from natural impulse. The natural, the carnal, is powerless to uplift, to beget sympathy, for it is the nature of natural things to resist each other. Man will never yield to, much less be inspired by, what is no better than himself. His dissatisfaction with the finite — his searching but fruitless seeking for happiness without alloy, proves that he will be influenced and ruled only by God, or by him who represents God. God alone can appease the ravenous hunger of the human heart.

Unless grace is the be-all and the end-all of our lives, unless we are impelled by the deep, abiding realization of Christ's Presence, we cannot be the chosen communicators of the gracious operations of the sacramental God dwelling within us.

Only when the natural dies in us; only when we live entirely to Christ and not to ourselves; only when He speaks and acts through us, will His effluence be a divine magnetism to draw and a divine power to save the souls of our brethren.

The life-giving God yearns to share His glory with us poor mortals, thus enabling us to cooperate with Him in casting and kindling the fire of His love in the hearts of others, making us thereby His privileged helpmates in the salvation of our neighbor. Were we docile pupils in the school of love, we would become most zealous apostles by reason of the supreme gift that we so often receive. Growth to "the measure of the age of the fullness of Christ"[22] is comparatively easy for the soul that is generous with God, that meets wholeheartedly the response of His unrestrained love with the glorious freedom of the saints. God is the sun of its own spiritual life. For others, such a soul is the striking manifestation of the efficacy of grace. Illumined by the light of the indwelling Christ, even in the darkness incident to the weariness and toil of earth's constant warfare, it anticipates its part in the sublime symphony of song, the eternal adoration that rises from the heavenly hosts to the Triune God.

[22] Eph. 4:13.

Chapter Three

∞

How faith will bring you closer to Christ

The mystery of the Real Presence throws into bold relief the doctrine of the Incarnation. It quickens our faith, and thus clarifies our understanding of this central dogma of Christianity. This is supremely important, because the Incarnation, in which the divine and the human are substantially united, lifts us up to God by developing in us a higher, supernatural life. Reflection on the Holy Eucharist will shed light on the Incarnation. Most striking is the resemblance between these two mysteries of unfathomable love.

First of all, in each mystery there is the union of the divine and the human. What excites our wonderment most in the Incarnation is that the God who fills all space and is not comprehended by it, whose infinitude we cannot grasp, should take a limited form in order to dwell in a human body. Marvel of marvels! The Eternal God with all His attributes enshrined in frail flesh, Christ becoming like man in all things save sin,[23] subject to human infirmities and dependent upon His creatures — the mystery of the Real Presence arouses the same wonderment.

Here again, Christ contracts Himself, so to speak, in order to identify Himself with the lowliest elements. What a union

[23] Heb. 4:15.

of two extremes — the sovereign majesty and omnipotence of God in a glorified state, circumscribed so as to adapt Himself to our limitations! In the Incarnation, Christ concealed the divine beauty of the Godhead in finite nature; in the Holy Eucharist, He veils His perfect divine and human natures with the appearances of bread and wine.

Another marvel of the Incarnation is the substantial union of two diverse substances, the human and the divine essentially distinct, the one unable to assimilate the other; a union of the infinite, and hence unchanging and unchangeable, with the finite, and therefore changing and changeable. God, being eternal, cannot change. But the human nature of Christ was mutable, for, says the evangelist, "Jesus advanced in wisdom and age and grace with God and men."[24] Although substantially united with the divine nature, the human nature ever remains human, ever maintains its separateness. The divine nature retains its identity, its infinite distance from the human, and its absolute, essential simplicity. Despite this, the two natures are indivisibly united in the person of Christ. The actions of the one are the actions of the other. When the Man speaks, God speaks. The Holy Name of Jesus can be predicated no less of the Godhead than of the manhood, because the person is one. While Christ could not suffer as God, it is as true to state that God died on the Cross as to say that the Man was crucified. We can truthfully affirm that Christ Jesus is from eternity, although we speak of His eternal generation only as God.

A similar wonder confronts us in the Blessed Sacrament — that is, in the transubstantiation of the changing and changeable

[24] Luke 2:52.

bread and wine into the unchanging and unchangeable God. The earthly elements, retaining only their appearances, are transferred from the realm of the natural to the domain of the supernatural, and are substantially changed into the Body and Blood, Soul and Divinity of Christ through the divinely taught words of Consecration. In the Holy Eucharist, faith reveals under either element the Second Person of the Adorable Trinity. The appearances, the color, the taste, the smell, the weight, and the extension of the two elements remain. The substance is wholly heavenly, supernatural, and eternal.

In the mystery of the Incarnation, we meet with the intimate coexistence of two natures substantially united in the person of Christ. In the Blessed Sacrament, we behold the same intimate coexistence, not of the substance, but of the appearances of the earthly elements, with the true, real, and substantial Presence of the God of love. In the Incarnation, the union is eternal; in the Holy Eucharist, it is temporal; but in both instances, the union is equally true and real. In the former, the union is substantial and personal, for there could be no Incarnation without the assumption on the part of the Divine Son of our human nature; in the latter, it is accidental — not personal, but sacramental.

Once more, how complete is the parallelism in the two mysteries, as regards the progressive growth to maturity of Christ as man in the Incarnation, and the gradual development to perfect spiritual symmetry of the grace of the sacramental Christ in the soul of the communicant. In the Incarnation, the human and divine natures were as truly, as perfectly united in the first instant of the miraculous conception of our Lord as they were when He had grown to man's estate. And yet what mystery shrouds the gradual unfolding of Christ's powers of mind and body, and their substantial and eternal union with His divinity!

There is a signal similarity to the Incarnation in the Mystery of the Holy Eucharist. Christ entering into us sacramentally adapts Himself to our limitations. The divine nature, united with a nature entirely unlike itself is, so to speak, cribbed and confined by the littleness of the creature. When He unites Himself with us, He gradually develops virtue in our souls after the manner of His own growth as man in "wisdom and age and grace," His sacramental life expanding by degrees until we become like Him.

Finally, hiddenness distinguishes both mysteries. The revelation of the Son of God in the Incarnation, His taking a human form, speaking and acting like a human being, but remaining practically unseen, unknown, and misunderstood by the creatures whom He had come to save; or the dim, slow recognition even of those enlightened by grace to discern Him, is a mysterious and accusing truth.

No less mysterious and accusing is the fact that He suffered His inward glory to be obscured by the overpowering outward world. It seems as if humanity as a whole was not worthy of a deep, vivid impression and recognition of His presence. But Christ ever strove silently and secretly to influence those who received Him not, veiling the Godhead lest its manifestation should be for them the occasion of chastisement, a more terrible condemnation.

He is the same hidden God in the Blessed Sacrament. His humanity as well as His divinity is invisible to the creature. Faith alone reveals Him.

Sight, taste, touch, in Thee is each deceived,
The ear alone is most safely believed.
I believe whatever the Son of God has spoken;
Than Christ's own word there is no surer token.[25]

So profound is the humiliation of the Savior's absolute hiddenness that many, for this very reason, deny the possibility of His sacramental Presence. His eucharistic life thus repeats His incarnate life. But, although hidden from our eyes, He manifests at times, as "in the days of His flesh,"[26] His omnipotence, so that those who are maliciously indifferent to His Crucifixion and death are so affrighted by the very Presence they outrage that they dare not approach Him.

With the prophet, let us cry out, "Verily Thou art a hidden God."[27] In the Incarnation and in the Eucharist, Christ shows Himself to the eyes, not of the body, but of the soul. Hence the caution of the Monk of Kempen: "Thou oughtest to beware of curious and unprofitable searching into this most profound Sacrament, if thou wilt not be plunged into the depths of doubt. 'He that is a searcher of majesty shall be overwhelmed by glory.'[28] God is able to work more than man can understand."[29] Too much curiosity, too close a scrutiny, too meticulous an examination, only baffle and confound.

[25] St. Thomas Aquinas (c. 1225-1274; Dominican philosopher and theologian), "*Adoro Te Devote.*"

[26] Heb. 5:7.

[27] Isa. 45:15.

[28] Prov. 25:27.

[29] Thomas à Kempis (c. 1380-1471; ascetic writer), *Imitation of Christ*, Bk. 4, ch. 18.

O sacramental God, increase our faith!

To perpetuate to the last syllable of recorded time His love among us — so undeserving of it — by His Presence on the altar, to compensate for the loss of His visible presence, to mitigate the anguish of separation, to be the pledge of our eternal union with Him, is a miracle of divine condescension. That the same God who assumed our fallen nature to be one with us, who wept over our sins,[30] who suffered for us mental and physical torture that defy description, should so humble Himself and, despite our neglect of Him, should remain with us — this is a love for which man has no name. The incarnate Christ has gone. "I go to Him that sent me."[31] But before He went, He said, "I will not leave you orphans."[32] He reveals the fullness of His life, which is love, to the children of the Church Triumphant. The same fullness, adapted to their capacity, He manifests to the children of the Church Militant.[33] Marvelous union of love and power!

Oh, who can conceive the joy that will be ours when Christ "shall rise to judge,"[34] if we have led our lives close to the Eucharist? How blissfully reminiscent will we be of the Holy Communions received, the Masses attended, and the moments spent before the tabernacle, when Christ will tear asunder the eucharistic veil and show Himself to us in all the majestic grace and perfect beauty of His divinity!

[30] Cf. Luke 19:41.

[31] John 16:5.

[32] John 14:18.

[33] The Church Triumphant comprises the members of the Church in Heaven, the Church Militant, the members of the Church on earth, and the Church Suffering, the members in Purgatory.

[34] Job 31:14.

Chapter Four

∞

The Eucharist can give your soul a glimpse of Heaven

For the God of infinite sanctity to dwell sacramentally in us is, in view of our sinfulness and myriad weaknesses, not only a profound mystery, but an inexplicable mercy. Strange and alien to our natural life is the blending of these two extremes. The contrast is not unlike that which exists between Christ and the appearances under which He gives Himself to us.

Were the Virgin Mother or an angel thus united with us, what a marvelous miracle it would be! But the miracle of miracles is the union of the God whom the Heaven of heavens cannot contain with a being of frail dust and ashes. If faith did not guarantee its reality, who could believe it? How can our finite nature, so feeble, so poor in virtue, with its countless imperfections, enthrone the God of almighty power and absolute perfection? But just as Christ associates Himself with the manifestations of bread and wine so that He may be accessible to us, so, notwithstanding the infinite contrariety of His nature to ours, He unites His greatness with our nothingness.

What a revelation of divine power! Thus restraining His communication, thus concealing His unimaginable beauty, He makes our reception of Him silent, peaceful, gentle, and restful. Advance as we may in holiness, however, we shall never unravel the mystery of this amazing union. Indeed, the more we progress in virtue, and the keener our spiritual sight, the more incomprehensible will be the mystery. Even in the world beyond, in the fullness of the glory that shall be revealed in us,[35] greater wonderment will seize us at the thought that the Eternal God did perform such a miracle.

This union has no parallel in the sphere of creation. Never has God given Himself to the creature so intimately, so entirely. This union is comparable only to the union of the divine and the human nature in the person of Christ. It is unique, constituting as it does for us an essential distinction from the world around us. It differs substantially from the union flowing from God's ubiquity, by which He is the preserver of all life, of the power of feeling in irrational beings, and of sensation, intellection, and volition in rational beings.

Nor is this union like that which exists between the heavenly hosts and their God. It is something more than all this. It is not merely the preservation of created life by one act of God's omnipotence, but the perpetual giving, the ever-renewed communication of Himself — Body, Blood, Soul, and Divinity — to the creature, mercifully adapting His infiniteness to finite capacity so that He, "God of God, begotten, not made, consubstantial with the Father by whom all things were made,"[36] may abide in man in oneness of life.

He gives Himself first to the soul. He then diffuses Himself throughout the body, becoming "bone of my bones and flesh of my flesh,"[37] so that even the mortal part of me experiences the closest contact with the God of love.

---

[35] Cf. Rom. 8:18.

[36] Nicene Creed.

[37] Gen. 2:23.

A glimpse of Heaven

The essential contradiction between Christ and us, between His divine and our human consciousness, is a truth whose content is inexhaustible. The difference between our sinful nature and His infinite holiness is far more marked than the difference between the full meridian splendor of the sun, and dense darkness. How can we reconcile such extremes? How can we associate what is so incomparably superior with what is so immeasurably inferior? How can we conciliate light with darkness?

It is Christ's boundless love for us in the Blessed Sacrament that accomplishes this miracle. Divine charity, eternally inventive, establishes a communication, a community of feeling, with the creature — the eucharistic God hiding Himself so that He may dwell in fallen nature. Ever active within us, He awakens an interchange of thought, an identity of desire, and a mutual understanding. We then begin to recite the very truth that He is our Brother, discovering, as He patiently abides in us, a ground of approach, a second home, until He finds His rest in us, with our sympathy, our love, and our companionship attuned to His, and our minds enlightened in order better to understand Him. Hence we yearn to satisfy His claims on our sympathy and our love, and to be one with Him in a common consciousness of mutual trust, with all differences gone, with our souls promptly obedient to His voice through full fidelity to grace.

As the realization of the power of this communication intensifies under the efficacy of grace, we become one with Him in thought and sentiment. This intimate fellowship with Christ, the source of joy, delights us and gives us peace and rest. This in turn is accompanied by increasing wonderment mingled with salutary fear, because the better we know Him, the more His presence fills us with awe, and the more His holiness haunts us with a lively sense of our unworthiness, which forces us to rid ourselves of all that is earthly, that we may welcome and entertain our God with all our powers, under the spell of the radiant beauty of His majestic Person.

Only when we harmonize our lives with the divine life within us does this union become a living reality. Christ will be the King of our hearts, the director of our pilgrimage, only if we are one with Him in thought, desire, and sympathy.

Again, we must accustom ourselves to His mysterious presence and the world created by it, however strange it is to our natural selves. With the entrance of the sacramental Savior into it, the soul becomes a veiled Heaven. Christ introduces into us a life sublimely and supremely supernatural.

As we deepen, by habitual recollection, the conscious possession of this marvelously mysterious life, our whole being is changed. We adjust ourselves to the charmingly attractive atmosphere of this new life. We see all things in a different light. With acute penetration we behold the passing events of earth. Our contacts assume a new coloring. A supernatural appreciation of duty, a purer, because more unselfish, love, wells up in us, enabling us to value persons and things as God appraises them.

Under the influence of this life, our fellowmen no longer appear to us what they were. Bound heart and soul by the natural, it is hard for us to conform this new supernatural relationship with the natural. It seems as if we are unknown to former intimates. And yet we dread to lose this new spiritual association with those with whom we were heretofore united by earthly ties. How to be true to both is the problem that confronts and perplexes us. We have completely changed our point of view.

Gradually, however, we realize that fidelity to the new life is the measure of our loyalty to the old. The new relationship, far from severing us from our former friends, has served only to cement our union with them. We are now living a higher life. We love with the love of Christ. The sweet constraint of this purer love has elevated and ennobled our natural love. We have risen to a loftier plane of virtue, with the horizon of our spiritual vision greatly enlarged. We now see things in their true relationship, with keener interest, replete with truer significance, because our souls have been purged of the carnal gaze through the life that has entered into us.

We behold with our spiritual eyes, as we have never beheld with our bodily eyes, all nature doing the will of God. We perceive the perfect harmony between the worlds of nature and grace, both converging, like rays of the sun, to a single focus — to Him, their Creator and Preserver, who causes the one to support and develop the other with the constancy of the sun, preserving and expanding to its ordained maturity the seed buried in the earth.

To harmonize and habituate ourselves to the Divine Presence within us, we should with wondering and adoring love converse with the eucharistic God, pondering the absolute certainty of the life that we possess and the effect it should have on the laws and habits of our lives. This introspective conversation with the hidden Savior will urge us to reduce to practice His faintest admonitions and His gentlest impulses, longing, as we muse on the reflected Heaven in our souls, to lead our earthly life in its brilliant light, in a truly heavenly manner.

A deepening of the spirit of faith will also help us to realize these two ends. We can attain this by earnestly trying not only to embrace, but to cling tenaciously to our indwelling God through a more docile correspondence with the grace of His Presence, soaring far above the snares of sense and the realms of reason into the regions of the unseen, and there living in the unshaken conviction of the truth most consoling: the limitless possibility of Christ's work within us.

Another means of accomplishing these two ends is practical devotion to the Holy Spirit, who wrought the miraculous conception of the Son of God, who was the divine communicator of His humanity. He hovers over the altar "at the awesome event, the evocation of the eternal, which is the scope and interpretation of every part" of the Mass; and, lavish of the grace of the sacramental Savior, He unites us with Him and inspires us with the determination to imitate more closely the life of Him who daily condescends to be born again for us.

Patience is likewise necessary to discipline, to strengthen, and to refine the soul, that it may concentrate wholly on God. Our fallen nature's incapacity for grace is the reason for our slow progress in virtue. Our tendency to sin is the greatest obstacle to correspondence with grace. We must, then, be patient with ourselves, ever remembering that God is all the more generous with His grace according to our gratitude or our correspondence with the present grace, for this is the infallible expression of our gratitude.

We are not therefore to despond because of our fitful growth in holiness even with the eucharistic God mightily at work within us, for the clouds of earth too often obscure the divine light, no matter how brightly it burns in the soul.

Our vitiated flesh is not the only reason for our failure to realize this state of spiritual understanding, because our very weakness made the Eternal God become man. Neither can it be due to the fact that the memory of former sins persists in haunting and affrighting us, for every Holy Communion, by a miracle of God's forgiveness, remits venial sin, and Confession removes mortal sin. Not any positive sin, but the soul's proneness, through morbid introspection, to dwell unduly upon its frailty because of its past transgressions, explains its discomfiture.

The vision of the sacramental Savior is blurred by the soul's excessive self-concentration. The soul thus underestimates Christ's infinite generosity, and not understanding, even imperfectly, the possibility of the coexistence of the infinite with the finite, it does not embrace His mercy and His love. Distrust, doubts, and scruples seize the soul, creating vague anxieties directly opposed to faith, and so depress the soul that it loses heart; and convinced that it, unlike others, is no longer the object of Christ's eternal pity, the soul plunges, through lack of faith and hope in its Master, almost into the abyss of despair.

Abandonment to God is the unfailing remedy for such a soul. Hidden though it may be by a cloud, the light nonetheless shines within it. In its strange helplessness, it should remember that "whom the Lord loveth, He chastiseth; and He scourgeth every son whom He receiveth."[38] Humbling itself

---

[38] Heb. 12:6.

"under the mighty hand of God,"[39] it will gradually be strengthened, and its love so deepened and purified by trial that it will rejoice to have been "accounted worthy to suffer . . . for the Name of Jesus."[40]

And so this enervating experience will become for the soul the groundwork of a childlike confidence in Him who "reacheth from end to end mightily and ordereth all things sweetly"[41] for His elect; and, patiently awaiting the Lord to deliver it, and desiring only the accomplishment of His will, it will hear the voice of Christ distinctly, and all its anxiety and fear will vanish, and the darkness will be dispelled like the morning mist fleeing before the warmth of the strong, brilliant sun.

No one has ever trusted in the Lord and been abandoned. This spiritual truism man instinctively forgets. Our love of God does not rise above our hope in Him. He can grant instantly — for grace works swiftly — what has been ardently asked for in the suspense and painful expectation of the years, which He may have decreed as a condition for His greater glorification. Darkness makes light all the brighter. "Power is made perfect in infirmity."[42] God delights to contrast infinite strength with infinite weakness.

Inertia and activity are so closely allied (the one is a form of the other) that their interchanging with startling speed is a fixed law. Realizing this, "in patience we will possess our

---

[39] 1 Pet. 5:6.
[40] Acts 5:41.
[41] Wisd. 8:1.
[42] 2 Cor. 12:9.

souls."[43] "Expect the Lord, do manfully, and let thy heart take courage, and wait thou for the Lord."[44] The very consciousness of our weakness, which emphasizes the sense of our helplessness, may be but the impetus to a fuller revelation of the quickening power of God's love.

[43] Cf. Luke 21:19.
[44] Ps. 26:14 (RSV = 27:14).

Chapter Five

∞

You can reach others through the Eucharist

∽

Every fruitful Holy Communion is a union not only with Christ, but also with our fellowmen. "We, being many, are one bread, one body, all that partake of one bread."[45] The spirit of self-oblation by which Christ gives Himself to us must, by eliminating — or at least controlling — our natural selfishness, unite us in the bonds of charity with others.

The sacramental God transforms us by making our thoughts and desires one with His. In proportion as their range expands, we may estimate the strength of our union with Christ and the members of His Mystical Body. The longing for perfect union with the eucharistic Savior presupposes the simultaneous yearning to be one with our neighbor. Only on this condition will Christ consummate His union with us. In this respect, the Blessed Sacrament illustrates the eternal life of the Godhead. Although there are three Persons in God, He is nevertheless essentially one. This perfect essential unity in plurality of Persons is the fathomless mystery that we love and adore. We tend to perfection according to our imitation of it. We reflect this life by the retention of our distinct personalities and our mutual relations with one another, while at the same time we are all bound together with Christ in one Mystical Body.

[45] 1 Cor. 10:17.

To realize its end, the Holy Eucharist must beget this union. For this Christ prayed when He changed the bread and wine into His Body and Blood. "I pray . . . that they all may be one, as Thou, Father in me, and I in Thee: that they also may be one in us."[46] This oneness of nature with countless diversities of distinct individualities is the culmination of the idea eternally in the mind of God, and constitutes our perfection. This is the burden of Christ's prayer in the tabernacle, the soul of His intercession in Heaven.

Holy Communion is the partaking of the perfect life of the eucharistic Savior. It is the mystical but real representation of the unity and trinity of God. As the three Divine Persons are one and the same God, so, in the reception of the Blessed Sacrament, we are united with Christ, and in Him, with the Father, in the unity of the Holy Spirit. Although possessing our individual personalities, like the Father, the Son, and the Holy Spirit, we are united with one another in one common ground of life, after the manner of the union of the three Divine Persons.

When Christ prayed for this union, His heart embraced the Church collectively, and Her members individually. He beheld His Mystical Body spreading throughout the world; and bestowing on it a sacrament that would establish every single soul in true relationship with every other, He would perfect it with a unity symbolizing the eternal unity of the Triune God.

Little wonder that the Holy Eucharist, uniting in sweet fellowship the members of Christ's Church, one with another, and all with Him who is their Head, is called the mystery of love. The Blessed Sacrament completes, therefore, the grand

[46] John 17:20, 21.

purpose of the Incarnation; for union of creature with creature, and of creature with God, is the fundamental idea of this overwhelming mystery. This union transcends time and space, linking us children of the Church Militant with the saints of the Church Triumphant and the members of the Church Suffering.

Here in a land of shadows, and with limited intelligence, we can but weakly comprehend our union with the world of spirits. But Christ in the Holy Eucharist rises above the conditions of our present state. Hence His union with us knits our souls with the saints in glory, and with the souls preparing themselves, both in Purgatory and on earth, for their eternal union with God. Although the souls in the world beyond, unlike Christ, have a fixed abode, they live their life in Him, the source of all life. The characteristic of this mysterious living communion, binding all in one, is its continuity.

Of this truth, as strange as it is thrilling, we have but a vague idea. When we receive our sacramental God, we experience, however feebly, the feeling of a bond of union. We are conscious of the pressure of the myriads comprising the kingdom of the Incarnation. We seem to share their common life. Our hearts seem to dilate with joy, and we rejoice in this dim consciousness of contact with the visible and invisible worlds.

We behold our brethren participating in this common life, and being drawn more closely to us by means of it. They are quickened afresh by the united charity of Heaven, earth, and Purgatory. We visualize the angels and archangels around the tabernacle in prostrate adoration, acknowledging by their fascinated homage their happiness at our exaltation to communion with the beatified Hosts, and even with the Blessed Trinity.

The Holy Eucharist, joining the world here with the world hereafter, embraces life's most comprehensive unity. At the moment of Holy Communion, we live in our own finite way the life that is, in all its glory, the joy of the saints. Our souls are kindled with the love that folds them with "the peace of God, which surpasseth all understanding,"[47] to the bosom of their Creator forever.

The same love that identifies the saints with Christ and with one another, likewise associates all who are truly Christ's with one another in heavenly harmony. Frequent Communion, with its gradual growth of grace, and consequent increase of this common love, so develops and so perfects this union that we imagine we are rapt into Heaven.

What will be the effect of this union? Under its gentle guidance, we will lead singularly supernatural lives, uprooting all those natural repugnances flowing from difference of character, divergence of opinion, and discrepancy of social standing, which too often separate heart from heart, as if men were born enemies and not brothers. The abiding conviction of this common life will so strengthen our faith and intensify our love as to draw all others to us, despite the marked variety of their distinct personalities, and one thought will rule our minds: the image of Christ, through the influence of His grace, assuming definite shape and form in the souls of even the least of our brethren, as well as in our own.

It follows, therefore, that we must be distinguished for the queenly virtue of charity, for the eucharistic King binds us to a mutual interchange of thought and action vitalized by love.

[47] Phil. 4:7.

Indeed, the essence of a sacramental life is union with Christ and our fellowmen, whether they are here or in glory. In the calm possession of this unity of life, and hence of love, disagreements that would tend to kill charity are forgotten, because the God of love reigns in the soul.

The altar is the school of this divine love. The Eternal Father, contemplating the image of His glory in us, His children, throws the mantle of His forbearing mercy over our weaknesses. Beholding such a sight, He seems to palliate the deformity of our nature, and to increase His love for us.

How can He do otherwise than rejoice in us in whom His Son chooses to rest? Moreover, through the triumphant power of His grace, He sees the glorious, eternal consummation of the indwelling presence. His loving acceptance of us through the reception of His Son is the heart of our hope of salvation in Christ. To realize this hope, we must be united with others, in imitation of the Savior's union with us and with every other soul in the state of grace. He is the source of the life of grace that flows into all the members of His Church, appeasing their hunger and slaking their thirst for justice,[48] unifying all, even as He is one with the Father in the bonds of eternal love.

Christ dwells in others as He dwells in us. His attitude toward us should, then, be our attitude toward others. The spiritual relationship effected between us and our fellowman should enlarge our vision to the extent of enabling us to overlook his faults, and broaden and deepen our sympathy for the disorders of his life. Worthily received, the Blessed Sacrament will rob life of its bitterness. It will inspire a supernatural considerateness,

[48] Matt. 5:6.

forbearance, and forgiveness — unknown to the natural man — which will grow with every Holy Communion.

The eucharistic God remains in the tabernacle to perfect our union with Him and with our brethren. What thought before and after Holy Communion would be more suited to our interested contemplation? We are united in a common consciousness of divine love, strengthened at the fountainhead of all strength, our souls replenished with the communicated fullness of Christ. Oh, if we realized this, how quickly all rancor, contention, and discord would vanish! How our lives in their tranquillity and peace would resemble the divine life of the God of the altar! Daily Communion will foster and perpetuate this unity, for our hearts, beating with the love of the heart of Christ, will long to extend this common fellowship in His life.

The perfection of this most precious fellowship should be the aim of every Holy Communion, so that externally there may ever issue from and return to us a love, a tenderness, and a compassion for every other child of God, the faint intimation of the fire of charity that burns within us, to preserve this common unity of grace.

This love, the unitive power of all God's works, we shall behold in its eternal beauty when grace shall have been crowned with glory, and we are forever associated with the marvelous unity of the life of our God — if, during our exile, we do nothing to hinder this oneness of life, which is the joy of our exile, and stamps us children of God's predestination.

Chapter Six

∞

How to give yourself completely to Christ

In the Holy Eucharist, Christ is both the Food of our souls and our Teacher and Model. Through the worthy reception of the Eucharist's sacramental grace, we commune most intimately with our God, and so become like Him. In Holy Communion, He teaches us the life that He wishes us to lead, its special characteristics, and the laws of its progress.

We may view Christ's life in the Blessed Sacrament under three different aspects, from which we may draw eminently practical lessons. We may consider His life toward the Father, in itself, and toward us.

In this mystery of love, Christ ever intercedes for us with the Father. He is our great High Priest, unceasingly offering Himself and begging forgiveness for our sins. With all the powers of His sacred humanity, He adores the Father, and longs with infinite longing to increase the Father's glory through the sanctification of souls. This intense devotion to the glory of the Father but echoes the inspiration of His life when He walked among us as our eldest Brother.

The eucharistic life of Christ is in itself wholly new. When He assumed our flesh, He became like us in all things save sin.[49] His growth, like that of every other human being, was

---

[49] Heb. 4:15.

accomplished by suffering and sorrow. It was wrought by trial both within and without, by the most agonizing of deaths, by His burial, by His wondrous Resurrection, and by His admirable Ascension. In the Blessed Sacrament, this onward progress yields to calm repose, to divine changelessness, in the full perfection of His glorified humanity. Christ in the Holy Eucharist, one with the Father, abides in the perfect peace of the completion of man's redemption. Impervious to inward change or outward unrest, proof against the ravages of time, Christ's life in the tabernacle is the same as His life at the right hand of the Father, replete with divine stillness.

For us, Christ's sacramental life is an act of continual self-immolation. In Holy Communion, He gives us His divine life. To do this, He conceals Himself in mysterious secrecy, hiding Himself in elements absolutely unworthy of the Godhead. But they truly illustrate His unspeakable gift to us of spiritual food and life, for He wills to thrill us through and through in one infinite largess of life, nourishing us body and soul with His own Body, Blood, Soul, and Divinity.

The more we imitate Christ's eucharistic life by frequent Communion, the deeper will be our insight into the laws governing it, and the stronger our conviction that our lives must be directed by the same laws. Our transformation by these laws will trace in our souls the image of the sacramental God.

Christ on the altar ever contemplates the face of the Father. As, in the days of His humiliation, He continuously sought to glorify the Father, so, in the Holy Eucharist He will, to the end of time, always yearn to glorify the Father through our sanctification. Those who, in union with Christ, lead sacramental lives, must be noted for the same zeal. For their own souls' welfare, they will adore Him; as mendicants, they will constantly beseech Him, cast all their care upon Him, and remind Him of their needs, their anxieties, their weaknesses, and their "wrestling . . . against principalities and powers, against the rulers of the world of this darkness, against the spirits of wickedness in the high places."[50] In all the difficulties of their oppressed souls, they will, with submissive sincerity, turn to Him for light, strength, deliverance, consolation, and peace. For the sanctification of others, especially those under their charge, they will importune Him for grace, mercy, pardon, and rest, so that they also may bear their burden with resignation to His will, and thus clothe themselves with His infinite strength.

Ardent lovers of the eucharistic God will acquire, by the grace of this sacrament, the peace of His life in the tabernacle. This peace is not the inertia resulting from the want of interior struggle or exterior conflict. It is not a negative but a very positive factor in our lives. It is born of self-conquest through daily mortification of every power of the soul, every sense of the body. As the life of grace grows within us, our natural restlessness and vacillation succumb to its sovereign sway.

Again, Christ dwells on our altars that we "may have life, and may have it more abundantly."[51] This life is mysteriously ours as often as we communicate. The sacramental God would have it animate our whole being. This we can do by keeping the eye of the soul sound; that is, by simplicity in our intention, and purity in our affection. "By two wings, a man is lifted

---

[50] Eph. 6:12.
[51] John 10:10.

up from things earthly; namely, by simplicity and purity. Simplicity ought to be in our intention; purity in our affection. Simplicity tendeth toward God; purity apprehendeth and tasteth Him."[52]

We are transformed by Christ only insofar as we progress in the imitation of the threefold aspect of His eucharistic life. Daily meditation will, with Christ's unfailing help, contribute mightily to our transformation.

A prerequisite for this spiritual sublimation is unlimited confidence in God's power. The fullness of grace can, if worthily received, carry the soul to the apex of growth in holiness. Where Christ alone abides in a soul, no height of holiness is too high for it to scale. We may have promised to be found faithless; we may have fought only to fail. Nevertheless, fidelity to grace will give us infinite strength, will fan to intensest fervor our love of our indwelling God, and develop to a rare degree our interior life with a constancy wholly divine. Christ dwells in us to unite us forever to Himself; for love dies if it is not one with its object.

We can mount spiritually to alpine peaks only through total self-extinction accompanied by a faith that moves mountains.[53] How tenacious we are of self! How narrowly and nervously solicitous about self! How self absorbs our thoughts!

Always and everywhere, self is most aggressive — in civil life, in temptation, and even in prayer. Self is the censorious critic of God's Providence. Self cuts our neighbor with its sharp angles. Self is the deadliest foe to progress in virtue.

---

[52] *Imitation of Christ*, Bk. 2, ch. 4, no. 1.
[53] Matt. 17:19, 21:21 (RSV = Matt. 17:20, 21:21).

Union with Christ is self-denial, self-sacrifice, and self-extinction. The eucharistic Christ cannot possess a soul enslaved by self-love. His death, and its memorial, the Blessed Sacrament, have virtually no meaning for such a soul, for "Christ died for all, that they also who live may not now live to themselves, but unto Him who died for them, and rose again."[54]

The Divine Lover in the tabernacle longs to diffuse His life. If we are to resemble Him, then love, which is His life, must so burn within us as to set on fire the world around us. "I am come to cast fire on the earth, and what will I but that it be kindled?"[55] Christ wishes us to create or renew this life in others.

To be His true disciples, we must not possess our sacramental God selfishly, but, like Him, we must willingly and generously sacrifice ourselves, be other Christs, in the unrestrained, perfect development and diffusion of His life of love. As love acts and reacts, our charity, especially toward those who need it most, through daily, thoughtful kindness, through a delicate anticipation, and, if possible, through relief of their wants — through spending ourselves and being spent for them — will determine the extent of our love of Christ and His love of us. The God of love cannot abide in a soul where there is no love of neighbor. "He that abideth in charity, abideth in God, and God in him."[56]

Rancor, discord, arbitrary caustic remarks about peculiarities of our fellowmen, or dogmatic judgment on their behavior,

[54] 2 Cor. 5:15.
[55] Luke 12:49.
[56] 1 John 4:16.

cannot coexist with the God who dwells in us only through love. Divine charity cannot but languish in our hearts if we rudely wound even the least of God's creatures. To appreciate the gravity of uncharitableness, we have only to consider God's unwearied patience with us, His meek tolerance of our sins, and the supreme gift of Himself when we return to Him. He cannot, therefore, possess a soul contracted by distrust, embittered by resentment, or poisoned by jealousy.

To receive Holy Communion according to the mind of Christ[57] is to lead a life lost in God. "As the living Father hath sent me, and I live by the Father; so he that eateth me, the same also shall live by me."[58] When the presence of the sacramental Savior within us crucifies our carnal selves and disengages our thoughts from earth, we will bear with our brethren and give to our contact with them the element that will mark our eternal communion with the saints. As, under the guidance of the eucharistic King, he runs the way of God's commandments, the communicant who fully corresponds with the grace of Holy Communion will so fuse his earthly with his supernal state, that his body will be on earth, but his soul in Heaven.

Christ suffered, died, and gives Himself in the Blessed Sacrament, to transform the creature and unite him to his God. Will such love find little or no response in our lives? Let us but profit by the grace of Holy Communion, and we will be one with Christ, and in Him one with the Father, realizing therefore the end of both Baptism and the Holy Eucharist, by which

---

[57] 1 Cor. 2:16.
[58] John 6:58.

we are created new creatures, by God, and in God. We will thus labor incessantly for the one thing necessary,[59] and be honored instruments in the hands of Christ for the salvation of others, one with them and Him, here and eternally hereafter.

[59] Luke 10:42.

Chapter Seven

∞

You can possess the joy of Christ

∞

Human apprehension cannot gauge the effect of one Communion, let alone frequent Communions. The Mass is the mystical revelation of Christ's death, Resurrection, and Ascension. In Holy Communion, we share in these eternally significant mysteries. The priest daily offering the Holy Sacrifice, renews bloodlessly the sacrifice of the Cross, for "Christ, rising again from the dead, dieth now no more; death shall no more have dominion over Him."[60] Christ has forever relinquished the trappings of death and assumed the raiment of immortality, a fitting reward of His life of sorrow and suffering and His heart-rending Crucifixion.

In receiving Christ, besides sharing in the infinite merits of His Passion, death, Resurrection, and Ascension, we are made one with Him through being nourished by the Bread of Angels. We shake off cosmic dust through the gradual working of the eucharistic Savior within us. Transported by the sacramental God who gladdens our souls with the glory of His presence, we become entirely His; we exchange earth for Heaven.

The whole life of Christ enters into us when we communicate. His life of contemplation, of action, of infinite patience, of eternal love, and of unearthly peace, is mysteriously ours.

[60] Rom. 6:9.

He, whose love for us could be satisfied by nothing short of the assumption of our nature, abides in us as God and man.

He dwells in us with His eternal yearning for the Father's glory, and His perfect conformity to the Father's will. He ever intercedes with Him for us, while pleading with us to serve Him lovingly and perseveringly. He purifies our love and beautifies our souls. With unflagging desire and intensified ardor, He petitions the Father for the gift of freer correspondence — on the part of His Mystical Body collectively, and its members individually — with the graces that He so generously bestows upon them; suffusing their souls with the joy that delights the heavenly hosts with rapture ever increasing and undying. Such is the life of the eucharistic Christ within us.

As the active principle of our spiritual development, He never tires of urging us to "approve the better things."[61] According to the sincerity of our devotion, He diffuses His life; He grants His gifts in proportion to our love of Him. What He desires most is that our lives reflect His indwelling life, that all our actions be convincing evidence of closest contact with Him. Our realization of the development of His life within us, and our living it, will be manifested by our joy or our sorrow.

We cannot consciously possess Christ without experiencing and spreading supernatural joy. True, it will be intermittent and somewhat changeable, unlike the joy that will be ours hereafter. And it will differ from (although it is akin to) the joy accompanying the possession of the Holy Spirit, who, opening the gates of heavenly happiness, and swelling the billows to immeasurable heights, serenely wafts the soul far above the

---

[61] Phil. 1:10.

mists and shadows of its earthly lot. But this joy, springing from the conscious possession of Christ, will lighten the burden of inward trial and soothe the irritation of outward pain. Sorrow can never depress a soul for whom Christ, dwelling in it, is a constant, instead of a fitful, reality. Faith waxes sublimely strong in such a soul — Christ absorbs the soul.

Sadness, paradoxical as it may seem, will tinge this joy. The heart will instinctively be overcome with poignant sorrow when the mind contemplates Christ, who challenged His bitterest enemies to convict Him of sin;[62] Christ, who is sanctity itself, substantially united with woefully weak mortals who have been defiled with sin so often. The reflection, too, on the possibility of sinning again after having housed the sinless Savior, of not realizing the ideal that His presence within us has every right to demand we realize, and the consideration of what it cost Him to redeem us, of our dullness in understanding His teaching, not to mention our miserable failure to square our lives with it — such thoughts will transfix the soul with an acute sense of sin, inspiring perennial penitence, and will level us to the dust with the knowledge of our unworthiness to enshrine our God.

Intermingled with this sadness will be a reverential fear of offending our Infinite Lover. It will stir our souls to their very depths with the dread that we may lapse into an old habit of sin, or that our tendency to commit a particular sin — a desire, for instance, to avenge an injustice, or a passion for the unsatisfactory pleasures of the world — may, despite the help of grace, swiftly betray us into the hands of our enemy and drive far from us our God and our all.

[62] John 8:46.

To further the sacramental life, we must banish this fear by growth in the love of Christ. God is love.[63] The Incarnation is a mystery of love that man will never fathom. In virtue of Christ's love for us, the worthiness of our reception of Him depends chiefly on our love of Him. Love is the one grace which, facilitating freer conformity to the will of God, enlarges and quickens the soul, and renders it more capable of the ever-increasing fullness of the life of the eucharistic Savior.

Our love of Christ is no stronger than our appraisal of His love of us. He longs for us; we must long for Him. He seeks us; we must seek Him. True, He awakens our yearning for Him; but ours it is to increase that yearning to its utmost extent and, aided by grace, to hunger for a still greater outpouring of God's most precious blessings. "Blessed are they that hunger and thirst after justice, for they shall have their fill."[64]

This ceaseless hungering for the closest intimacy with the unseen yet ever-present God of the Eucharist will give us patience in our efforts to "mortify the deeds of the flesh by the Spirit,"[65] and will be our mightiest armor against the world and its seductive pleasures. The more our desires keep pace with the expansion of Christ's life within us, the dearer will be our vision of it, and the more thoroughly will we enter into complete accord with His designs for us.

Again, for the full development of His life within us, the soul enlightened by the Divine Presence must nourish its spiritual energies by constant contemplation of its Infinite Lover.

[63] 1 John 4:8, 16.
[64] Matt. 5:6.
[65] Cf. Rom. 8:13.

In a mystery eliciting from the creature the highest and purest faith, the soul's prayer should be: "Lord, increase my faith";[66] for as faith grows, the vision enlarges with greater grandeur.

What a power against temptation would this vision be for our souls if we beheld it with a look of enduring, concentrated expression so that we might live our lives in its divinely illumined splendor! With what consummate ease would we sanctify ourselves and scatter the seeds of virtue all around us! As we walked in the wondrously brilliant light of the God within us, come what might, the heartening consciousness of our Divine Guest would inspirit us to live for Him alone, in the newness of life, peacefully, and restfully, and would make for us a veritable reservoir of spiritual strength against our enemies.

Inseparable union with man was the goal of the Incarnation and is the reason for Christ's life in the tabernacle. On the altar, He watches over us with love unquenchable. To requite this love in our own finite way, we must, with the full measure of Christ's life working with us, ever strive for the attainment of that indissoluble union, constraining the God of love, the center of all true life, to draw us wholly to Himself, that our lives here may, however imperfectly, adumbrate the joy, the peace, and the glory that will be ours when, with the heavenly hierarchy, we shall chant the eternal hymn, "Holy God. Holy and Mighty One. Holy and Immortal One. Have mercy on us."[67]

---

[66] Cf. Luke 17:5.

[67] The Trisagion, a hymn used in the liturgy of the Byzantine rite.

Chapter Eight

Patience will pave your path to holiness

※

The disparity between the ideal and the real is necessarily great. The fact that the sacramental life develops slowly, and the communicant's failure to realize fully its sublime end, may be, especially for the soul eager to grow in holiness, a fertile source of disappointment and discouragement. For such a soul, a study of the reasons for this striking disparity will be most heartening.

The greatness of the gift cannot be overestimated. We will not be able to receive in Heaven more than Christ gives us on earth. The same God who nurtures our souls here, will fill them hereafter with bliss untold. The Infinite compasses the finite; the Creator absorbs the creature. Man lives in God, and God lives in man, but man is lost in God. Hence it is evident that the indwelling life can progress only slowly. This is one of its essential features.

Although in Holy Communion we are at once united with Christ, His power within us develops gradually. Progress is a fundamental law of creation, and the higher the life, the slower the progress. The plant does not mature suddenly. It must follow the strict, unbending, universally applicable law of growth. The masterpiece of the painter is a work wrought by slow, persevering labor. Harmony, which underlies all art, is but the gradual blending into one of diverse elements. All natural transformations are therefore essentially slow. Immeasurably slower is the change from the natural to the supernatural. Christ Himself, who was sinless, grew gradually because He assumed our flesh. Can we, who are often burdened with the intolerable weight of sin, hope to do otherwise?

Nor will the eucharistic God alone transform us. He requires our free, generous cooperation. Only by stimulating our higher faculties can we imitate Christ's life. There is a decided difference between possibility and actuality, between the capacity for this life and its possession.

This difference may be seen all around us. The almost-breathing statue lies hidden in the crude marble until the sculptor strikes the block with his chisel and fashions it as he wishes. The natural qualities of the voice are quickened into charming action only through constant exercise under a consummate master, until they satisfy the exacting demands of the severest critic. The gift of accurate, eloquent expression, capable of casting a spell over the most learned, is the direct result of slow, careful reading and persistent, accurate writing. Genius will soar highest when a mighty stimulus sets in motion its latent energy. The lifeless thought can never impress like the living word. The development of a gift is necessary for its perfection.

The most remarkable spiritual endowments follow the same principle. A pointed illustration of this thought is the preaching of St. Peter. Eloquence was his, but a cowardly fear stifled its expression. Only when the Spirit of love, the fire of that divine love that "casteth out fear,"[68] entered his apostolic

---

[68] 1 John 4:18.

soul, did he, with magic persuasiveness, enlighten the most educated and win souls to Christ. Sometimes individuals crushed with sorrow evince almost superhuman strength and, undismayed by suffering that can be felt but never described, rise to heights of moral heroism.

The sacramental life obeys the same law. Although Christ dwells in us with His Body, Blood, Soul, and Divinity, in order that His life may develop, may permeate our souls, and may direct our thoughts, words, and actions, the sacramental life must have circumstances favorable for its development, just as the plant needs sun and rain to grow to maturity. Without such circumstances and conditions suited to its growth, that life will never enrich us with its heavenly store; it will abide in us with the mere possibility of its infinite power, and we will be unconscious, not only of its greatness, but of its very existence.

Apart from the fact that we are sinners, our state of probation hinders the expansion of the eucharistic life. Hampered by the flesh, the soul cannot breathe freely and copiously the atmosphere created by Christ's presence. Natural corruption ever struggles against the fullness of its development. Furthermore, our daily venial sins, committed with monotonous regularity, with sickening spontaneity, are the reason why the indwelling God fails to produce in us more prolific spiritual results.

Too often we are at the mercy of ungovernable anger. We have little control of our thoughts and desires. We allow our imagination to wander capriciously. Old, sinful impulses are encouraged by an overwrought fancy noted for its creative power. Inordinate ambition for worldly renown may throw us into turmoil, tossing us hither and thither, and torturing our souls rendered tremblingly sensitive by the presence of the eucharistic God. Because of these inward disturbances, the life-giving power is practically dead within us.

Difficulties from without may also impede the fullness of sacramental development. A friend may wield over us an influence not altogether spiritual. The tongue, the eyes, and the ears may mingle too intimately with the outward world and completely paralyze the action of the hidden God upon our souls. Oversolicitude for the good things of earth may so master us as to awaken no response to the eloquent pleading of the sacramental Savior for the consecration of our lives to Him who has given Himself to us. It is, therefore, luminously evident that self-control is indispensable for the comprehensive action of Christ within us. Through the habit of self-discipline, our inward vision must focus upon, and our outward gaze issue from and converge to, the indwelling God. Unmortified self will neutralize the effect of the Divine Presence in the soul. Only in the soul at ease in the peace of self-mastery, solitary in the multitudinous world, silent in the presence of its God, will the Life of all life develop most fully.

The habit of brief, spontaneous prayer will help us to conquer self. A brief prayer repeated again and again will give us recollection by directing our thoughts to the greatness of our Guest. If the recipient repeatedly exclaimed after Holy Communion, "My God and my all!" — lingering with every repetition on the meaning of each word — how quickly he would overcome his ruling passion! What strides he would make in the science of the saints!

A corollary of the habit of such prayer, just as essential to the self-discipline of the soul, is secret conversation with the eucharistic God. The realization of the intimacy of the union between Him and ourselves will result in a oneness of feeling that will notably affect our spiritual life. It will embolden us to ask more confidently for an increase of His grace. It will help us to unburden ourselves of our peculiar difficulties and trials; will rid us of apprehension, the gloom of uncertainty, and the anguish of doubt, and will strengthen and calm us in our efforts to accomplish the great work of life.

The mingling of our thoughts and desires with those of Christ will animate us with that divine sympathy that will guide us through the midst of our deadliest enemies so securely that we will be able to say, with the royal psalmist: "The Lord is my light and my salvation; whom shall I fear? The Lord is the protector of my life; of whom shall I be afraid? If armies in camp should stand together against me, my heart shall not fear. If a battle should rise up against me, in this will I be confident."[69]

For the soul ever recollected by brief, spontaneous prayer and silent communion with God "all things work together unto good."[70] Such a soul "finds tongues in trees, books in the running brooks, sermons in stones, and good in everything."[71] The action of the eucharistic God within the soul expands it to full spiritual stature, and urges it to do great things for Christ. Inspiring the soul with the living conviction of the supernatural, this action revolutionizes the aspect of the natural. Like clay in the hands of the potter, the soul's life is molded and controlled by the God ruling within it.

---

[69] Ps. 26:1, 3 (RSV = Ps. 27:1, 3).

[70] Rom. 8:28.

[71] William Shakespeare (1564-1616; English playwright), *As You Like It*, Act 2, scene 1, line 12.

In the sustained power of the state born of repeated acts of recollection, wedded to its intellectual consciousness of the in-dwelling God, and with its most ordinary mental, moral, and physical activity dominated by the eucharistic King, the soul becomes a fit soil for the growth of the virtues of its Lord and Master. The human loss entailed by the overcoming of itself and the world is swallowed up in the sweetness of its secret conferences with the hidden Christ. The soul has exchanged the shadow for the substance, the temporal for the eternal. It has become the child of God's predilection. It has already begun its unending fellowship with the Christ veiled within it. It has anticipated, although dimly, the joy that no man shall take from it,[72] when the soul will be one with its Eternal Lover.

Our soul, however, has to surmount two obstacles that may distress it beyond words. Immediately after Holy Communion, we may be touched to tears with the sense of Christ's presence. But suddenly, the realization that the sacramental Savior possesses us may become a mere recollection. Then it is that we must remember that sensible fervor is not religion, but its fitful, accidental accompaniment.

Perhaps we may be utterly unconscious of our loving God. Humble trust in the province of Him who numbers the hairs of our heads[73] must now be our sole stay and support. The God of the Eucharist would, by this drastic discipline, exercise and thus strengthen our faith. He would, on Calvary, not on Tabor,[74]

---

[72] Cf. John 16:22.

[73] Matt. 10:30; Luke 12:7.

[74] Tabor is the mountain on which Christ's glory was revealed before some of His disciples; see Matt. 17:1-2; Mark 9:1-2 (RSV = Mark 9:2-3).

entirely banish from us every trace of self, that we may live for Him alone.

The other obstacle our souls may find it even harder to surmount. We may be saddened because the Blessed Sacrament has produced no felt change in us. Calmness and composure will return to us if we but realize that sanctity is most solid when its hidden power shows itself in the ordinary, the insignificant, the commonplace. This is the surest sign of the progress of the eucharistic life. Holiness is most beautiful in the midst of the most uneventful. Few are called to do the extraordinary for God. All are called to be faithful in that which is least.[75] Very little skill is necessary for the painter to depict the crude outlines of the face. The sculptor readily cuts in the broad, bold lines of the statue. But it is the delicate retouching, the fine rechiseling, that bring out their superb beauty.

So, too, the unimportant events of our daily lives are the perfection of the edifice of sanctity. The minute care by which we restrain our looks, words, and actions; the vigilant supervision that compels us to check the effusions of our nature; the unobtrusive acts of self-suppression — these apparent trifles perfect the soul by completing in it the likeness of God.

What spiritual riches would have been ours had we corresponded more fully with the graces of so many Holy Communions! And yet, our very spiritual inaction should soften our souls with a "sorrow that . . . worketh penance steadfast unto salvation";[76] that will make them, to their utmost capacity, susceptible to the complete unfolding of our sacramental God.

[75] Luke 16:10.
[76] 2 Cor. 7:10.

Chapter Nine

You can keep Christ's presence alive within you

Theologians have debated whether Christ would have assumed flesh had man not sinned. The same question may be argued about the Holy Eucharist. Was the Blessed Sacrament instituted to restore to man what he had lost by the Fall, or was it the means divinely ordained for the greater perfection of the creature? It is hard to believe that the dignity to which man was raised by the Incarnation could have followed only from his sin. It is equally incredible that the Sacrament of the altar was given merely to return to man what he had lost. The view that makes the Holy Eucharist the instrument for communicating the life of the Incarnation with a view to the greater perfection of man seems the more cogent. There would indeed have been no restoration of fallen nature, but there would have been no need of restoration. To perfect the creature by conforming him wholly to his God, to strengthen and sustain him against the enemies of his soul — such appears to be the more convincing reason for the institution of the Blessed Sacrament.

According to this view, how magnanimous was Christ in giving His "flesh for the life of the world!"[77] What a comprehensive idea it conveys of the nature of this glorious Sacrament!

[77] John 6:52 (RSV = John 6:51).

Irrespective of sin, granting its power of remitting venial sin, the compelling motive for its institution was to unite man with his God by a union such as existed before the Fall.

This view is supported by the manner in which Christ gives Himself to us. We receive Him "who . . . bore our sins in His Body upon the tree, that we, being dead to sins, should live to justice";[78] and we receive Him without the faintest trace upon Him of the sins that He bore for us, and which so destroyed His beauty that He became "a worm, and no man, the reproach of men and the outcast of the people."[79] His sacramental presence is adorned with the eternal beauty of His glorified humanity. Serene calm has succeeded the raging storm.

A comparison between the reception of Baptism and that of the Holy Eucharist will demonstrate the truth of this view more clearly. When we, through our baptismal sponsors, promise to renounce the Devil, with all his works and pomps, our future struggle against sin in its alluring guises, against our passions, and against the Devil in his myriad shapes and forms is the substance of our pledge of allegiance to God. The promise anticipates the dangers to salvation and the necessity of warfare and alert vigilance, as, with the help of grace, we fulfill our course. The Holy Eucharist is the life of our regenerated souls.

This is the dominant idea of this masterpiece of God's love. Sin and the strife against it are abolished. For sin and the Divine Presence are essentially contradictory, and therefore, mutually exclusive; sin must not come between God and the creature. Their union in this sacrament cannot be overshadowed by sin.

---

[78] 1 Pet. 2:24.
[79] Ps. 21:7 (RSV = Ps. 22:6).

You can keep Christ's presence alive

The reception of the Blessed Sacrament is, so to speak, eternal life begun in us where sin dare not enter. After Holy Communion, we must fight against sin, but when we are receiving Christ, the black clouds of sin are not to dispel the sunshine of our inconceivable joy. It is as if sin had never touched our lives.

The same idea underlies our preparation to communicate. Sin must be banished before we presume to approach the banquet table of the Lord. We must be at peace with God before we receive Him as our Divine Guest. Hence Confession is divinely prescribed to fit the soul for a worthy Communion.

This view is not at variance with the fact that Holy Communion remits venial sin. Christ's power to forgive sin is most positive and efficacious in the Sacrifice in which He daily dies a mystical death for sinners. This consoling truth is, however, not the *leit motif*, but the minor chord of the Mass. The heart and soul of this mystery is the Savior's lavish giving of Himself; the subsidiary idea, the cleansing and offering of the regenerated soul, that the Divine Solitary may enter a living temple in which He will delight to dwell. Christ's infinite longing when we receive Him is to possess the soul entirely; to behold, therefore, sin no longer in us; and the only object of the Father's heavenly vision is to see His well-beloved Son in complete possession of the soul. It is the unspeakable union of love between the purified creature and God, its purifier. It is earth wholly cleansed, meeting Heaven in all its unsullied purity.

A serene sense of blessedness should pervade our souls at the moment of Holy Communion, for all that Heaven has to give is ours. In receiving the sacramental God, an eternity of joy is ensured for us who have become one with Him. Into a union so holy and so intimate, of the soul with the eucharistic Christ, sin must not intrude. For that instant, the knowledge that dust and ashes are housing the God of infinite sanctity is what masters the soul.

How thorough the triumph of grace over sin! How tranquil the soul in the midst of life's distracting cares! What brilliant supernatural light, which cannot be obscured, illumines the soul! How miraculously effective each reception of this inspiring divine power is as an incentive to serve God with renewed, indescribable fervor! Every Holy Communion marks the beginning of a truer, more perfect relationship with Christ and our fellowmen.

To be united with us in time and eternity is the one desire of the eucharistic Savior. Were we to reciprocate this desire, we would experience even between Holy Communions a foretaste of Heaven. Our hearts would beat with love, in unison with the Sacred Heart. The joy that earth knows not would flow from our fellowship with Christ. The eternal peace that is in no small degree the happiness of the saints, would wondrously calm the soul, no matter what the excitement of its earthly sphere of action. Virtue, ever maturing because of the influence of the Divine Guest, would recreate us spiritually. If the grace of this sacrament operated according to the will of Christ, immeasurable would be our progress in the fine art of living, by reason of the acting and reacting of this holiest of fellowships.

The same peculiarly affectionate, calmly confident interchange, the all-pleasing effect of the intimate union between us and our God, would unite us to our brethren, and we would instinctively feel that the sacramental God has graciously accepted the love of our hearts and theirs; the Eternal Father beholding in all, only His Divine Son, entirely sinless. It would seem as if we were transported to Heaven, whence we proceed to fulfill our earthly destiny, and again wafted there to enjoy Christ, no longer veiled to our eyes. Purely supernatural, because sweetened by the love of the eucharistic King, would be our relation to others if we were all of one mind with regard to this adorable mystery, and if this consciousness were revived whenever we communicated. The Savior dwelling in all of us would be the acknowledged definitive law of life, making us sensitive even to minute imperfections.

Bearing in mind these truths, we should, after each Holy Communion, reflect with the reawakened powers of enlarged spiritual vision, on the perfectness of our nature as it existed in the mind of God. Our effort to conform to the divine ideal will then become habitual.

Despite our multiple weaknesses, we are endowed with the capacity both to receive and to manifest continual impressions of the perfectness of the life embodied in our Head, Jesus Christ. The marvelous end of our existence is to imitate our Model, Christ, and hence with Him to glorify the Father.

God, with love eternal, willed not only our creation but also our perfection. He thus willed wholly to transform us in accordance with the perfectness of the life of Christ. The formation of Christ in us, therefore, was and is the object of His infinite yearning. Sin opposed our reception of this perfectness of life. To remove this impediment, the glory of the Incarnation had to be dimmed by the terrible giving of the Savior as a sacrificial victim. The God-Man willingly endured the physical agony, the withering sorrow, the shame, and the desolation of His Passion and death, that He might behold us and dwell in us as if we had never offended Him.

To accomplish this design of infinite love should be our absorbing aim, until grace has finished its work in our souls, when we shall be thrilled with the conscious, eternal possession of our God.

Chapter Ten

How to receive Christ with love

∞

In Holy Communion, we touch and taste our Lord and our God. A very significant sentence of St. Augustine, in which he records Christ's words to him, defines the chief effect of eating the Bread of Angels: "Thou shalt not change me into thine own substance, as thou changest the food of thy flesh, but thou shalt be changed into mine."[79] There is not, and there never can be, a closer union. The reality of Christ's Presence is a fact founded on His infallible word and almighty power. But bewildering is our perplexity when we try to ascertain the mode of His eucharistic indwelling. The nearer He approaches to us, the more incomprehensible He becomes; the greater our effort to understand, the more profound our obscurity. When our minds strive to progress beyond the limits marked by faith, they are baffled and confounded. The divine brilliance of light surrounding our guest impairs the soul's vision.

As their Creator, God abides in creatures. Man cannot be independent of God. For the creature to attain both his natural and supernatural ends, the Creator must dwell in him. Even irrational creatures fall under this essential law of creation. God is everywhere: by His being or essence, because He

---

[79] St. Augustine (354-430; Bishop of Hippo), *Confessions*, Bk. 7, ch. 10.

is the cause of all being, all existence; and by His knowledge, because "all things are naked and open to His eyes";[80] by His power, because all things are subject to Him. "In Him we live, and move, and have our being."[81]

But the Incarnation inaugurates an entirely new mode of the Divine Presence. Through this mystery, man becomes one body with Christ in the embrace of a common nature. Holy Scripture beautifully unfolds the eternal import of this prodigy of divine love: "God so loved the world as to give His only-begotten Son; that whosoever believeth in Him may not perish, but may have life everlasting. For God sent not His Son into the world to judge the world, but that the world may be saved by Him."[82] "This is eternal life: that they may know Thee, the only true God, and Jesus Christ, whom Thou hast sent."[83]

In this wholly new manner of the Divine Presence, how low Christ descends to exalt the creature! St. Paul's words to the Philippians on this subject are sublime in their simplicity: "Let this mind be in you, which was also in Christ Jesus: who being in the form of God, thought it not robbery to be equal with God: but emptied Himself, taking the form of a servant, being made in the likeness of men, and in habit found as a man. He humbled Himself, becoming obedient unto death, even to the death of the Cross."[84]

---

[80] Heb. 4:13.
[81] Acts 17:28.
[82] John 3:16, 17.
[83] John 17:3.
[84] Phil. 2:5-8.

As an earthly king, realizing that he is God's representative, and having at heart therefore the dearest interests of all — but especially of the poorest of subjects — as such a one conceals his royal raiment beneath attire as shabby as theirs, in order to be more accessible as he distributes his gifts to them, so the King of kings wraps in fallen nature the eternal glory of His divinity, to raise man in new bonds of love to a higher life, to give him the gift greater than which God Himself cannot give.

So, too, the words of Christ: "If anyone love me, he will keep my word, and my Father will love him, and we will come to him, and will make our abode with him"[85] put the soul into a relationship with God far closer than that by which the Creator is everywhere in His creation. God dwells in man in a special way, it is true, because man, being rational, is the only creature who can know and love the Creator. But the Divine Presence connoted by the Incarnation differs essentially from its consequences. In this instance, Christ is the almsgiver of Heaven's largess, revealing Himself under conditions entirely new, and in a manner that, until the fullness of time had come, could not be realized.

By this mystery, man's sin was forgiven, the supernatural life of his soul restored, and his nature justified and elevated to the most loving companionship with God. The creature was endowed with the capacity for growth into the likeness of his Savior so that, by the acquisition of His virtues, the mind that is in Christ should also be the mind that is in him.

But even beyond the restoration of man's nature to its primal supernatural righteousness, and his ability to reproduce

[85] John 14:23.

the virtues of Christ in his soul, there is, through the Incarnation, the living consciousness of the union between God and man, and the joy accruing to the creature from the personal love of Christ, dwelling in such close intimacy with him. This is the crowning glory of this preeminent mystery — just as the harmonious blending of colors, producing the most delicate tints and finest shades, completes over and above the rough outlines, the masterpiece of the artist.

All these marvels coalesce in the Holy Eucharist. This sacrament was instituted to confer on us, not merely particular graces, but all the gifts of the life of the incarnate God as well. Never has God revealed Himself with such energizing fullness. Such a revelation does not, however, contravene the bestowal of a definite grace in answer to a special request. Christ can manifest Himself to us in the manner best suited to our spiritual development because He is the infinite archetype of all the forms of holiness; the source of sanctity in all the varied expositions of its comprehensive unity.

Reflection on these stirring truths will impel us to receive Him with a love that will satisfy His yearning to be one with us. He must be one with us in order that, sharing His eucharistic life, and profiting by its treasures, our weak, changeable nature may be transformed and our faculties supernaturalized, and we may be fashioned into His likeness.

What Christ by His sacramental presence does in us, we should do in the world around us. As He transfigures us with His grace, we, too, must elevate and ennoble all who come within the sphere of our influence. We fall short of the divine purpose in the institution of the Holy Eucharist if we fail to dispense the beneficent effects of the Life of all life. Conscious of the marvelous expansion of its power, we will do everything we can to requite the love of Christ for us by always being His representatives in the world's wilderness of sin.

This thought, that we must be other Christs, should inspire our words and actions. Briefly, we must glorify Christ by emptying ourselves for others, as He glorifies the Father by emptying Himself for us. What a mission of purest love would be ours if we daily endeavored to kindle in the souls of our brethren the fire of love which our Savior came to cast on earth, and longed so ardently to see kindled!

How else can we make possible the eucharistic life of our Lord and Master in our own souls? Christ came to restore to His Father the souls of sinners. Only by continuing this work, only by love of our neighbor, will we be saved, for our sacrifices, and the helpfulness of our charity for others, will decide our eternal destiny.

" 'Come, ye blessed of my Father, possess you the kingdom prepared for you from the foundation of the world. For I was hungry, and you gave me to eat; I was thirsty, and you gave me to drink; I was a stranger, and you took me in; naked, and you covered me; sick, and you visited me: I was in prison, and you came to me.' Then shall the just answer Him, saying: 'Lord, when did we see Thee hungry and fed Thee; thirsty and gave Thee drink? And when did we see Thee a stranger and took Thee in? Or naked and covered Thee? Or when did we see Thee sick or in prison and came to Thee?' And the King answering, shall say to them: 'Amen I say to you, as long as you did it to one of these my least brethren, you did it to me.' "[86] The doom

---

[86] Matt. 25:34-40.

of the faithless will be ours if the eucharistic life ends only in selfish possession.

Our expression of responsive love and gratitude after each Holy Communion should be to glorify the sacramental Savior by the revelation in all our dealings with others of the effect of our union with Him.

Chapter Eleven

How to sanctify
your daily duties
through the Eucharist

⚭

There is a vast difference between spiritual and sacramental Communion. We receive Christ spiritually by an act of faith. We receive Him sacramentally when we partake of the Sacred Species.

Christ in Heaven is received by the children of the Church Triumphant under His proper species; that is, through perfect charity, or the most intimate union with Him. They receive Him neither sacramentally, by actually eating His Body and drinking His Blood, nor spiritually, by an ardent desire to do so, because the faith that motivates such a desire has become for them knowledge.

As the two modes of reception, spiritual and sacramental, differ, so does our conscious response to them. In receiving Christ spiritually, the soul experiences the sense of a gentle interchange of thought between itself and its God. Immeasurably stronger is the effect of sacramental Communion. The Infinite Lover appears to overpower the devout soul, and so conscious is it of His presence that it surrenders itself to His love. Such a soul feels that it is no longer its own, but under the sway of omnipotence.

Here, a question naturally suggests itself: How long does the fullness of the sacramental presence last? To assert that it perdures for life would be to deny that the Holy Eucharist is our daily bread, and would be inconsistent with our nature as finite, mutable mortals. If one Holy Communion sufficed for life, our time of trial would be an anticipation of Heaven, when our souls will be so transformed, so glorified in the rapturous consciousness of their eternal union with God, as to be invulnerable to change.

At the moment of Holy Communion, we have a very definite sense of the complete possession of Christ — a calm, heavenly absorption of His divine life quickens our souls. But if this condition continued, it would not accord with our spiritual development, which, because we are finite beings, is gradual; and the Holy Eucharist would not be the pledge of eternal life.

In every worthy Communion, grace is increased in the soul; however, although we advance in virtue according to our cooperation with the sacramental Savior, on returning to the level of our ordinary duties, we experience a change from the full consciousness of closest union with Him to virtually the bare knowledge of having received Him. From this we are not to conclude that Christ has withdrawn from us. Even though we lack that feeling of fullness of grace that is ours when we receive Him, we are still one with Him. The floodtide of grace has not ebbed from us, but only subsided within us, producing its salutary effects the more strongly, the more lovingly we correspond with it; but this grace works silently and in secret.

This consideration gives us a deeper insight into the meaning of Holy Communion. We may define Holy Communion either as the reception on the part of the finite creature of the infinite God, or as man so united with his God that he is lost in Him. We approach, as it were, to the very Godhead through the humanity of Christ. We feed on Christ and yet are changed into Him. We are united with the Father through the Divine Son, "the brightness of His glory, and the figure of His substance."[88]

In order that we may be able to receive Him, our Lord seems either to circumscribe His infiniteness or to enlarge our hearts. Both definitions conform to the mind of the sacred writer. In the eucharistic union, we may conceive ourselves as little children trying to empty the ocean into a tiny hole, or as souls launched upon its bosom, and intermingling with its vast and mighty life.

How poor, how inadequate, how impotent, are words to describe the union of Christ with ourselves, and of ourselves with Christ — the sacramental God entering into dust and ashes! The human mind cannot know God as He is. "No man hath seen God at any time."[89] "No one knoweth the Son, but the Father; neither doth anyone know the Father, but the Son, and he to whom it shall please the Son to reveal Him."[90]

We cannot fathom the mystery of the true, real, and substantial Presence of Christ within us, now truly our own. The Eternal God, infinite in power, dwelling in His finite, helpless creature! Overwhelming thought! In every Holy Communion, we taste the supernal sweetness of the divinely communicated life as it pours itself out in tidal waves of supernatural strength and the limitless riches of Christ's blessings.

To live our lives in the sustained consciousness of this transcendent union is a duty to which we should devote ourselves

---

[88] Heb. 1:3.
[89] John 1:18.
[90] Matt. 11:27.

with increasing earnestness. The effect of the realization of the Divine Presence within us will purify our love of Christ, instill into us greater reverence for our indwelling God, inspire us with a wholesome fear that will quicken our sensitiveness to the least shadow of sin, develop a constant watchfulness over our feelings and their expression, enable us to wrestle unceasingly with our frailty and conquer our natural inclinations, discipline every power of the soul, mortify every sense of the body, and make us live to Him alone by dying to ourselves.

But to benefit most by the grace of this sacrament, that our lives may, however imperfectly, illustrate the divine life of the God of the altar, serious preparation for Holy Communion is indispensable. How tensely expectant we would be, how moved to recollection, dispelling every distraction, were we assured that when we entered the church to receive Christ, He would show Himself to us as He is! Yet can we question His word, which guarantees the reality of His Presence even though it is hidden from our eyes?

The fullness of divine glory is there as truly as in Heaven, but concealed under the earthly elements. If we are absolutely convinced of this truth, it will be the pivot around which our preparation will revolve. Burning with love, we will then exultingly exclaim, "Behold, Thou art present with me on Thine altar, my God, Saint of saints, Creator of men, and Lord of angels!"[91]

The calm, joyous realization that we possess Christ will also animate our thanksgiving after receiving Communion. Even if we are not vividly conscious of the presence of our

---

[91] *Imitation of Christ*, Bk. 4, ch. 1.

Divine Guest during the performance of our daily duties, it will influence us both interiorly and exteriorly, sanctifying the most trifling commonplace of our unobtrusive lives. It will urge us to imitate His eucharistic life, cost what it may, for the spirit of Christ will sustain us, and His light will not only illumine our own souls, but will also enlighten those "sitting in the darkness and shadow of death."[92]

Unless Holy Communion makes us one with Christ, the light of His sacramental presence in us cannot shine before our fellowmen. "My Beloved to me, and I to Him."[93] If we consciously bear Him about with us, His divine strength will overcome our inconstancy, which, pandering to the human in us, is the greatest hindrance to this union. "Who will grant unto me, Lord, to find Thee alone, and to open unto Thee my whole heart, and to enjoy Thee even as my soul desireth; and that henceforth none may look upon me, nor any creature move me, nor have any regard to me; but that Thou alone mayest speak to me, and I to Thee, as beloved is wont to speak to his beloved, and friend to feast with friend. This I beg, this I long for, that I may be wholly united with Thee."[94]

---

[92] Cf. Luke 1:79.
[93] Cant. 2:16 (RSV = Song of Sol. 2:16).
[94] *Imitation of Christ*, Bk. 4, ch. 13.

Chapter Twelve

∞

The way to give thanks after Communion

∞

In Holy Communion, we are alone with God. Blissful solitude, where the soul can rise above the world, and with mute wonder, with breathless adoration, bask in the eloquently solemn silence of the Divine Presence! In this solitude, where the voice of God is most articulate, we can support and sustain our conscious weakness with the strength of the personal revelation of the sacramental God. Our doubt and fear will vanish before Him who alone can satisfy the insuppressible longings of the soul. With inconceivable generosity, Christ can grant all we ask and more, for the incapacity of man cannot limit the bounty of God. In adapting Himself, however, to our limitations, He veils His eternal glory with the appearances of bread and wine, so as not to overpower us.

The period of thanksgiving should be for us, hushed in the bosom of the hidden Christ, one of rapt recollectedness, of wondering contemplation that marvels at the infinite perfections of Him whom we have received, of faith that renders these perfections visible, and of speechless amazement at the greatness of the gift. Our every faculty should be under the absolute control of the awe-inspiring Presence, the ears of our soul docilely attentive to the voice of God, the eyes of our soul enamored of divine fascination, feasting upon our best Benefactor.

Nor will our contemplation be confined to the time of thanksgiving, as if we were beholding but a fleeting shadow of earth. The vision of the reality of the Divine Presence will perdure, with our whole being under the dominion of the in-dwelling God, who penetrates into the deepest depths of our souls and, with divine love, swallows up our poor, finite life in His infinite, eternal life. We will not look at Christ fitfully, but will be captivated by the beauty of the vision through habitu-ally beholding it. The darkness of our fallen nature will flee before the light within us, and, in the brilliant brightness of its divine radiance, not only will flaws of character, even the most trivial, be disclosed, but our entire being will be morally transformed by the eucharistic God.

The light and power of the vision will, if the soul concen-trates on it, produce this one marvelous effect of Holy Com-munion. In this sacrament, Christ plainly shows His goodness to the soul, so that it may rise under its compelling influence to a life of permanent union with Him, and be conformed to His image.

To gratify this dominant yearning of the Sacred Heart, the soul must divest itself of oversolicitude, divorce itself deci-sively and completely from attachment to the outward world, and direct its thoughts to Christ alone.

Largeness of desire should characterize our thanksgiving. In the gift of Himself, Christ includes all other gifts. Convinced of this truth, we can be bold with God. We can presume on His kindness and try to exhaust His generosity. We should banish all distrust of the Infinite Lover.

Nor must we have any misgiving, now that we possess Christ, about our ability to advance rapidly in virtue, for with

God all things are possible,[95] and to become a saint is the reason for our creation. Our expanding energies are not to be contracted by the thought, suggested by the Father of Lies,[96] of old vicious habits; the copious flow of grace is not to be retarded by the sorrowful recollection of its former sins. The fear of sinning again, and therefore of severer judgment, must be supplanted by the yearning to advance in virtue because of greater grace received. Into this mystery of undying love, gloom born of sinful experience should not enter.

On the contrary, our soul should be joyously courageous and calmly confident, rising, as it embraces God in the fullness of fervent faith, up to the happiness of Heaven, even though we had before Holy Communion been desolate with fear and wasted with sorrow. Christ will surely answer such faith, because this largeness of desire imitates His own boundless beneficence.

A ready, spontaneous, practical correspondence with grace, the effect of lively faith, will accompany largeness of desire. Possessing God, the soul will grow in the consciousness of an increasing capacity for divine light, and will slowly acquire, within the scope of its limited powers, the knowledge of the full greatness of God's love. Mental growth is measured by the prolonged contemplation of a particular study or a definite object. The increased mastery of a science depends upon the yearning for its acquisition.

The more the mind progresses in truth, the more enlarged and developed becomes its capability for receiving more truth.

[95] Luke 1:37.
[96] That is, the Devil; John 8:44.

As the horizon of knowledge widens, the mind's power to grasp increases, and the desire for more knowledge keeps pace with the mind's greater power of intelligence.

The same truth is seen in the spiritual order. The more we desire to know God, the clearer will be our vision of Him. As the vision enlarges, so do the capability and desire of the soul, and they will continue to grow through their mutually responsive action upon one another.

How truly unique is the eucharistic revelation to us, despite the impenetrable veil that shrouds our sight! In the Blessed Sacrament, Christ dims the brilliance of the eternal glory of His manifestation by hiding His presence. And yet what an alluring paradise is the lingering radiance of this communication to the pure soul! God's goodness in all its unblemished beauty is not concealed from the creature. This is all the soul needs to be convinced with peculiar force and cogency that one Holy Communion can make us a saint.

For this gift that rifles the treasures of omnipotent power, an acknowledgment of our utter unworthiness, actuated by sincere humility, is our best act of thanksgiving especially when we contemplate the vision of the infinite perfections of Christ that is mercifully vouchsafed to us. Like the sacramental God who, because He is eternal, cannot change, the revelation of His light in the soul is constant. Constancy, therefore, in the service of God will develop the soul for the greater diffusion of this light. The world's enticing pleasures must not obscure the vision, or dim the light, by chilling the ardor of our desire ever to follow it by growing conformity to Him whom it manifests.

If we walk in the reflected glory of the sanctity of Christ within us, He, our eucharistic Lover, will illumine us so that we may instinctively detect the treachery of the angels of dark-ness, and He will "direct our feet into the way of peace,"[97] until He lifts the veil and we enter into that eternity of bliss that is incapable of exhausting the beauty of the vision.

[97] Luke 1:79.

Chapter Thirteen

∞

How to pray in front of the Blessed Sacrament

∞

In the Holy Eucharist, Christ is not only the food of our souls, but also the companion of our exile. The human heart yearns for the sweet consciousness of companionship. The Divine Presence in the tabernacle fully satisfies this natural longing, for God alone can fill the heart. Actual sight is not necessary for the felt nearness of those we love. The mere sign of their presence is enough to fire the imagination and thrill the mind. It elicits all the precious associations, all the pleasurable sense of intimate fellowship, causing them to loom up before us in their vivid, substantial reality.

Christ fulfills His promise of continued companionship by laying hold of this universal law of His own implanting in our nature. In the Blessed Sacrament, through the unmistakable signs of our Lord's nearness, we experience the most thorough enjoyment of His companionship. To recognize His presence, we need not behold Him. His word, although He conceals Himself from us, proves His sacramental reality. The elements that veil Him to mortal eyes make Him accessible whenever we wish to converse with Him.

If we are prayerfully recollected in our audiences with our Lord and Master, He soothes our troubled souls into placidity by the atmosphere of His proximity to us. In Holy Communion, His loving embrace fills us with a joy that will, if we reciprocate His love, efface every other feeling by its superior ardor. But even in our moments before His eucharistic throne, in the stately silence of His gentle, gracious, genial presence, we are spiritually refreshed with His light and strength.

Silent and loving before Him, we are absolutely certain of His hidden reality; more certain than they who, in the days of His flesh, beheld and touched His body, which curtained the magnificence of the Godhead. With the eyes of faith, we see Him, not disfigured and clouded by the weaknesses of human nature, but shining with heavenly light in the grandeur of His beauty and in the perfection of His attributes.

To be so near our God, so rapt in love before Him, is to receive His most coveted blessings. As, when He walked the earth, He went about doing good,[98] so, from the tabernacle, He dispenses love, joy, mercy, and peace. All that concerns us is to Him too deep, too precious for words. He cannot therefore send us away without some emanation of His humility, His obedience, His meekness, His self-denial. He best knows our needs, and will, if our faith is strong, supply them, or at least lighten the burden oppressing our hearts. And once within the circle of His divine attraction, we will leave Him either with our petitions answered, or with courage to suffer patiently.

In our visits to the Divine Solitary, we can with intense devotion prepare ourselves to receive Him sacramentally. Poor, wretched, miserable, blind, and naked, we cannot alone make ourselves fit for the reception of our God. He must clothe our souls with the wedding garment of divine grace, and adorn them with virtue.

---

[98] Acts 10:38.

How to pray in front of the Blessed Sacrament

As we kneel before the eucharistic Savior, the Eternal Father will draw us closer to His Divine Son. Christ will so influence us as to bring out the best that is in us. The Holy Spirit will calm us with the peace of God, and thus remove the obstacles to our loving advance in intimate conversation with the sacramental King. Our very nearness to Christ will dispel our diffidence at the thought of too hasty an approach to the God who has found sin among the angels. Breathing the spiritual air of the tabernacle, illumining our souls with the light reflected from His earthly dwelling, strengthening our wills for conflict with temptation, deepening our faith in His almighty power, and purifying our desire to love Him more unselfishly — how can we better prepare ourselves to receive our God with a fervor that will ever inflame us with eager enthusiasm in His service?

The peace of soul that is ours in our moments of adoration is a blissful exaltation above the turmoil of time, an anticipation of the eternal peace of Heaven. Our union with the eucharistic worshipers, the myriad hosts of angels that surround the tabernacle, adoring in Heaven as they gaze forever on His soul-stirring divinity, humbly prostrate before Him in His sacramental lowliness as He hides the beauty that would overwhelm us — what is this but paradise on earth?

Thus raised above the visible, we can forego its claims and honor Christ for His own dear sake. We can compensate for the irreverences of those who believe, but do not realize, the mystery of His Real Presence, and for the profanations of those who absolutely deny it. If we love Christ, we will gladly spend ourselves trying to repair the dishonor which He so patiently endures in the sacrament of His love. The conscious recognition of what He suffers will help us to increase our love of Him.

Our reparation does not remove the injuries, nor do we absolve the offenders by offering our love as compensation for their want of love. But heart speaking to heart in understanding sympathy gives to the heart's desires an additional value. Only too tragically verified, in our day, are the words of the evangelist: "He came unto His own, and His own received Him not."[99] In the anguish of His rejection by so many for whom He died, Christ turns to souls who love the tranquillity, the eternal calm, of His eucharistic humiliation. As they tell Him of their joy just to be near Him; as they beseech Him for greater grace to communicate more worthily; as they pour out their love for Him — love ever intensifying with the frequency of their Holy Communions — as they invite the angels around the tabernacle to join in their act of thanksgiving for this divinely gracious gift, their love and their gratitude will touch His Sacred Heart, and will make amends for the heartless unconcern, the chilling disregard, of His thoughtless creatures.

When the world is cold to Christ, and questions with superficial, destructive criticism the truth of His sacramental presence, while He continues to dwell with infinite patience in a desert of forgetfulness, where ingratitude so abounds, and to bless those who outrage Him, our loving reparation may be best appraised by the withering disappointment that the sacramental Savior daily experiences in those who seem to delight in driving Him, their God, far from them.

---

[99] John 1:11.

How to pray in front of the Blessed Sacrament

God is always lavish of His love. To enhance our appreciation of His goodness, and therefore add to our happiness, He adorns His gifts. The natural world demonstrates this truth. The gorgeous beauty of the landscape; the golden glory of the rising and setting sun; the colors, which only the Divine Artist could blend, of the rose, the lily, and the violet; the human body with its admirable grace of movement; the attractiveness of the human countenance; the inestimable pleasure of true, loyal friendship — these, which are not necessary for existence, but which so embellish and heighten the enjoyment of life, since they are its distinctive charm, all testify to the magnanimity and tenderness of God's love.

The same truth is applicable in the institution of the Blessed Sacrament. Christ, in this prodigy of divine ingenuity, besides being the food of the soul, and the pledge of eternal life, is also our companion in all the hardships of earth. The joy of His loving, silent, yet consciously felt, affectionate companionship — the harbinger of our intimate, perfect, eternal union with Him — is a superadded blessing, as if this were the only reason for this overflow of divine love.

O eucharistic God, deepen our supernatural consciousness of Thy infinite generosity. Consume in us all that is worldly. Purify wholly our interior and quicken our higher faculties, so that we may better appreciate this supreme expression of Thy love for us. Kindle in our hearts a love that will meet the advances of Thy love and associate us now and forever with Thy deepest source of life.

Chapter Fourteen

How to purify your love through the Holy Spirit

∞

The Spirit of God is as closely associated with the Blessed Sacrament as with the Incarnation. A comprehensive view of the Holy Eucharist, therefore, necessarily includes a study of the operation of the Holy Spirit in this miracle of divine love.

In unity of aim and extent of action, and in the ends attained in both mysteries, there is perfect harmony between the Divine Son and His Holy Spirit. But their revelations and their methods of operation are different. This perfect harmony, this difference coextensive with the whole life of Christ, and its fruit, the kingdom of grace, is discernible in the Blessed Sacrament.

In this mystery, the Holy Spirit is even more hidden than Christ. At the altar, He unites the human and the divine, and through His help, we communicate worthily. As, in the Incarnation, He wrought the miraculous conception of the Son of God, so, in the Holy Eucharist, He is the worker of the mystery, the maker of the sacrament. The sacramental Christ gives Himself to us, and we give ourselves to Him only by the ministry of the Holy Spirit.

Meditation on His hidden character in this mystery will refine our reverence and purify our love for Him. Although coequal with the Divine Son, He plays only a ministerial part in the sacrament of love.

He did likewise in the mystery of the Incarnation. How complete His self-effacement as He glorifies Christ in the assumption of our flesh! And as He unites us with the eucharistic God in Holy Communion, what secrecy, which serves only to emphasize His love for us, hides His action! Holy Scripture marks the beginning of the manifestation of His love and power. "The Spirit of God moved over the waters."[100]

The first revelation of the Holy Spirit in the material order reflects His work in the supernatural domain until it flowers in human nature by enriching it with a dignity capable of intimate union with God. The initiatory stage of His action may be seen in His work in souls, enlightening, reproving, and strengthening them — inspiring, for example, the prophets to preach and thus fill fallen man with wistful longing for the coming of the Redeemer. His bestowing on Mary of the fullness of grace,[101] and so fitting her to be the Mother of the Messiah, culminated in the acme of omnipotence, the supreme miracle of the Incarnation.

Nor did His work end here. He was the silent and secret agent developing gradually the human soul of Christ. At the Savior's Baptism, He hovered over Him[102] and, with His gifts, perfected His human nature. He also shared in the Resurrection and in the immortal glory of Christ's risen life. In the mystery of the Holy Eucharist, He blesses the material elements with the most perfect of all blessings by changing them into the Body, Blood, Soul, and Divinity of our Lord, and multiplies

[100]Gen. 1:2.
[101]Luke 1:28.
[102]Matt. 3:16; Mark 1:9-10; Luke 3:21-22.

His sacred humanity with the celebration of every Mass. This is the practical meaning of the invocation of the Holy Spirit in so many of the preparatory prayers said by the priest about to offer the Great Sacrifice.

Christ's infinite condescension and the richness of His gifts to us vessels of clay[103] are impressively revealed in the concordant divine energy of the eucharistic God and His Holy Spirit. In both the Blessed Sacrament and the Incarnation, the Holy Spirit, by His self-effacement, glorifies Christ, and Christ, by making His humanity depend upon the operation of the Third Person, glorifies the Holy Spirit. Indeed, throughout His earthly life, the God-Man would do nothing unless under the direct influence of the Holy Spirit's quickening power. St. John teaches this truth: "It is the Spirit that quickeneth; the flesh profiteth nothing."[104] According to the beloved disciple, Christ's flesh, which He gives for the life of the world,[105] becomes that life only through the eternal action of the Holy Spirit.

He is just as active in preparing us to communicate. The elevation of the soul at Baptism, by which it becomes a new creature, a partaker of the divine nature, a child of God, and an heir of Heaven, is the gift of the Holy Spirit, and it unites the soul so intimately with Christ that St. Paul says to all Christians: "You are the Body of Christ, and members of member."[106] In Confirmation, He strengthens the life given at Baptism. And while this sacrament, unlike Baptism, is not necessary for

---

[103]Cf. 2 Cor. 4:7.
[104]John 6:64 (RSV = John 6:64).
[105]John 6:52 (RSV = John 6:51).
[106]1 Cor. 12:27.

the reception of the Holy Eucharist, the sevenfold gift of the Holy Spirit,[107] which it confers on the soul, completes the soul's spiritual capacity for union with Christ in the sacrament of His love.

In Holy Communion, the life of Christ and of the Holy Spirit enters into us, and forms and fashions Christ in our souls by making us one with Him. The Holy Spirit perfects in us this mysterious transformation. He is the Spirit of love, and therefore a unitive power. He unites the Father and the Son in the bonds of eternal love, for He is the mutual love of both. He overshadowed Mary,[108] uniting the human and the divine in the person of Christ, and He is the link that binds all in one body to Christ.

Of ourselves, we cannot communicate worthily. We need the help of the Holy Spirit. Even though we approach the altar free from mortal sin, He must sharpen our spiritual apprehension and inflame our love to intense ardor, that Christ may find in us a more beautiful habitation every time we receive Him.

The sacramental God has a divine right to expect on our part after each Holy Communion an intensification of our gradual growth into His likeness. As often as we receive Him, He would have us burn with the desire for greater progress in virtue that will manifest itself in an irrevocable detachment from the world and a more unselfish love of Him, grounded on the conviction of our nothingness and consequent sore need

---

[107]The seven gifts of the Holy Spirit are knowledge, wisdom, understanding, counsel, fortitude, piety, and fear of the Lord; see Isa. 11:2.

[108]Luke 1:35.

of Him. With greater joy will He abide in us if He beholds us by degrees assimilating His life, resembling Him in virtue by more complete conformity to His will. Christ will unite Himself most intimately with us if we are constant in our effort to imitate Him.

And all this is the effect of the direct operation of the Holy Spirit, who beautifies our souls with His holiness, and adorns them with His invaluable gifts. Being one with Christ, He traces in us the image of our Savior, for only by His power does the mind that is in Christ become the mind that is in us. Thus does He unite us with the sacramental God in the bonds of a common love. And because He is the Spirit of love, He stirs to the depths the love of the eucharistic God, and moves us to reciprocate it whenever we approach the banquet of the Lord.

St. John, speaking of Christ, says, "Of His fullness we all have received."[109] He who, in the Incarnation, filled the sacred humanity with the fullness of the Godhead, fills our tainted humanity with the Body, Blood, Soul, and Divinity of the God of ineffable sanctity.

Reflecting, before Holy Communion, on the essential, intimate association of the Holy Spirit with the central mystery of our Catholic Faith, we will beg Him to remove far from us whatever would impede our reception of the fullness of the grace of this sacrament. We will do more. With an ardor that dilates our hearts with exquisite joy, we will constrain Him to ennoble our thoughts and desires so that we may embrace Christ with a faith that moves mountains, and with a love supremely sacrificial. Then will we glorify our hidden God, and

[109] John 1:16.

our souls will be His home until the shadows flee away, and we return with the garnered fruits of infinite, eternal love, to contemplate forever the inexhaustible beauty that we adored under the eucharistic veil.

Chapter Fifteen

You can live
each moment
in God's presence

∞

A eucharistic life is the fullest development of the supernatural life. The sacramental Savior is its essential informing principle. Under His divine inspiration and direction, we do His will with the vivid realization of His presence in our souls. A eucharistic life not only apprehends Christ as the source of grace, but also bears the consciousness of personal union with Him, and the conviction of His living and life-giving power.

Through His presence in us, we become the means of communicating His infinite life, dispensers of His mysterious work within us, organs most holy, to reveal Him to those who know Him not or have forsaken Him.

The change produced in us, by which we freely submit to the absolute dominion of the eucharistic God, involves, besides the consciousness of His presence, the recognition that we must exemplify Him for others, especially for unbelievers, by ever giving outward expression to His operations within us. Such a change will infuse into us a sanctity that will so discipline the senses that they may not betray the soul; that will so control the imagination, the intellect, and the will, that we may use them only for the honor and glory of God — in a word, our lives will reflect the personal union of the two natures in Christ, the eucharistic King being to us what the Godhead is to His human nature. The mind that is in Christ will then be the mind that is in us, and His influence upon our lives will resemble the influence of the Father upon His life.

Because God rules man by love, He has made him free. How we use our freedom will determine our progress in virtue. If our wills are, in every event of life, one with the will of the indwelling God, we are standing on the rock foundation of holiness and perpetual self-renunciation; we are free with "the freedom wherewith Christ has made us free."[110]

But to be spiritually valuable, our self-surrender must be permanent; and on this point we should bear in mind that neither our unconsciousness of its action nor our failure fully to cooperate with Christ disproves its reality, for a habit is no longer the object of consciousness, and our fallen estate presupposes trivial temporary lapses. After all, the infinitely merciful adaptation of the sacramental God to the imperfections of our fallen nature is simply the alliance of infinite strength with untold weakness. As one of the consoling effects of the Holy Eucharist is the remission of venial sin, Christ abides with us until we, by mortal sin, turn violently from Him to the creature.

As man, Christ was heir to all the manifest faultiness of our flesh, sin excepted. He tasted mental and physical pain in all their withering, blighting, gruesome features, for He was the "man of sorrows and acquainted with infirmity."[111] He was rejected by those for whom He was to die. Like us, He was tempted. His soul was clouded by the darkness of sinful humanity in the crisis of His agony on the Cross when the Eternal Father hid His face from Him. But although subject to our

[110]Gal. 4:31.
[111]Isa. 53:3.

humiliations, He ever possessed the full consciousness of the Godhead. Our venial sins and imperfections may also weaken the sense of the Divine Presence within us, may eclipse the light shining in our souls. Or to test our faith, Christ may seem to withdraw from us; but He remains with us until we abandon Him by serious sin.

And who can estimate the effect upon the soul keenly alive to the indwelling presence? Even a superficial study of the degrading bondage of the flesh will reveal our imperative need of the strength of Christ within us as we fight our way to eternal life. What a restraint the eucharistic God exerts upon our sinful tendencies! If we are left to ourselves, sin in its multiple development will wreck and ruin us. Living in a corrupt world, and having the seeds of sin sown in our nature at birth, we are powerless against its false philosophy. Our ruling passion never sleeps.

Without the sacramental Savior, the soul would be the prey of demons. He is ever active thwarting the propensities of our fallen flesh, calming excitable, wicked emotions, and overthrowing the enemy the instant he attacks us. His light is a necessity of our earthly warfare as we wrestle with the angels of darkness; and only with His divine power can we conquer the hosts of Hell. He is our heavenly Sentinel controlling our thoughts and desires, ever alert lest we sink under the sudden or protracted attacks of temptation.

But the eucharistic Christ does more than restrain our sinful tendencies. In union with the Holy Spirit, whose temples we are,[112] He expands the soul's faculties so that it may be

[112]1 Cor. 3:16, 6:19.

conformed to His image as He gradually unfolds Himself to its enraptured gaze. Thus, through His Holy Spirit, does He develop in the soul the eucharistic life. Under such divine guidance, the soul's progress in the knowledge and imitation of Christ may be almost incredibly rapid. Directed solely by its God, it possesses the counteracting antidote to worldliness, and with divine chivalry it overcomes its worst — because its most insidious — enemy: unmortified self.

Under the spell of this wondrous world of truth, beauty, and sanctity, the soul's whole being is, by degrees, so transformed by Christ that it walks in the newness of life, reflecting the light shining so brilliantly within it. The will of God it docilely obeys; in the perfection of its conformity to it, it lives for Him alone. His divine nature weaves itself into every fiber of its being, making it one with Him.

Like nature's mightiest forces, Christ accomplishes this perfecting work silently and secretly. We behold it only in its results. So noiselessly and invisibly does the Divine Presence act in the soul that, although we observe in our conduct something beyond our mortal selves, we are prone to identify it with the workings of our human side; although we die to ourselves and live only to God, we associate the effluence of the supernatural with the outflowing of the natural. "The life . . . of Jesus may be made manifest in our mortal flesh,"[113] but the divine within, and its revelation without, will be veiled by the human.

This law must obtain until we have "shuffled off this mortal coil."[114] Were we not subject to it, life would hold no

[113] 2 Cor. 4:11.
[114] William Shakespeare, *Hamlet*, Act 3, scene 1, line 56.

interest for us. We could not fulfill the duties of our calling if we were constantly aware of the ceaseless miracle within us. If the Divine Presence continually showed itself through our nature, the world's thronging demands would have no meaning for us. A life of faith would be impossible, and hence our probation would lack the element on which rests our hope of salvation.

But the fact that Christ works so silently and secretly in us that we cannot distinguish between His operations and our own, is no excuse for our failure to lead eucharistic lives.

We shall give ourselves, heart and soul, to the full possession of Christ if we are thoroughly convinced that in Holy Communion He, the Eternal God, enters into our souls with His Body, Blood, Soul, and Divinity — in other words, if we realize what we believe. For self-surrender to Christ is born of a faith that compels the soul consciously and willingly to cleave to its Divine Guest. Interwoven with and flowing from such faith is a habit of prayer that penetrates the eucharistic veil, and thus accentuates the soul's longing to be formed completely after His image. Only when Christ is, by habitual recollection of His presence — and consequently of our inseparable union with Him — the sole Ruler of our lives, will they answer the end of the institution of this, the greatest of the sacraments. Then, and only then, will we lead eucharistic lives.

Chapter Sixteen

∞

Three ways to give
yourself more completely
to Christ

∞

In Holy Communion, the action of Christ's love and the reaction of our own constitute the fullness of our joy. We are not to be the languid beneficiaries of Heaven's best gift, but we must partake of the Bread of Life, and graciously welcome the God of our hearts, with religious earnestness that quite masters us, with pure and stainless souls in which the waves of trial and trouble roll under the surges of our joy, and with no strange, regretful consciousness of some barrier dividing us. As Christ gives Himself to us, we must give ourselves to Him, with the sublimity of faith and devotion, in an interchange of loving desires and mutual gratification.

Self-oblation is the essence of the mystery of the altar. The Sacrifice of the Cross is mystically but really renewed in every Mass. The same Victim offers Himself to the Father, presenting to Him the merits of His Passion and death with the living efficacy of their infinite satisfaction for the sins of mankind.

Our Lord offered Himself at the Last Supper and on Calvary, and ever offers Himself in Heaven, for sinful humanity. These three oblations are mystically repeated in the Mass.

In the Cenacle, Christ offered Himself when He said over the bread: "This is my Body, which is given for you," and over the wine: "This is the chalice, the new testament in my Blood, which shall be shed for you."[115] He thus anticipated His death. The offering was complete, for Christ sacrificed Himself by a free act of love.

While the oblation in the Cenacle was without constraint, violent external compulsion marked the Sacrifice of the Cross. In the Mass, the words "This is my Body; this is my Blood," which formed the substance of the offering in the Cenacle, are repeated, and they have the same effect, for the same Lord and Victim, placing Himself in human hands, offers Himself to His Eternal Father. Daily on the altar, Christ dies mystically through the miraculous words of Consecration. The Mass is our Calvary where the Divine Son, immolating Himself as He did on the Cross by perfect obedience to the will of the Father, dies a sacramental death through the external ministry of His human instruments.

The oblation of the glorified Christ is also repeated at the altar. His eternal intercession in Heaven comprehends every act of His mortal life of self-extinction. So closely united are the two that the heavenly offering is, as it were, the completion, the perfection, of the earthly sacrifice, and the Mass the projection, the extension, of Christ's eternal oblation. Thus are joined the visible and the invisible kingdoms of the Incarnation, with the intercession in Heaven embracing and exalting the offering of earth through the union of the earthly with the heavenly priesthood in a marvelous manifestation of eternal love.

The Mass is the focal point of these three oblations where Heaven and earth, time and eternity, meet; where Christ folds

[115]Luke 22:19-20.

to His heart the creature, and where the creature becomes the human tabernacle of his God. Sinners that we are, we share in this threefold offering and become "a chosen generation, a kingly priesthood, a holy nation, a purchased people."[116]

So intimately related, even though bound by the bonds of fallen nature, with these three inexpressible offerings, we should give ourselves to Christ, who daily gives Himself to us, and who alone can make our oblation acceptable; and thus complete the mystery of the eucharistic sacrifice in the mutual act of self-surrender. In the Mass, Christ is wholly ours; therefore, we should be entirely His. The sacramental oblation will then be a common act of reciprocal love and deep devotion, the union of the infinite with the finite, of divine love with human love, the power and beauty of Christ's glorified humanity recreating our sinful nature.

What a blending of extremes in every Holy Communion! God surrendering Himself to man; man surrendering himself to God! Man relinquishing his misery, and receiving in return the gift, so undeserved, of purest, freest, most disinterested love!

From the nature of Christ's self-oblation, we can learn what ours must be if we are to imitate His life.

Christ's offering of Himself in the Cenacle was without external pain. He expressively anticipated His immolation on Calvary by changing bread and wine into His own Body and Blood, Soul and Divinity, and giving them to the Apostles. It was the voluntary oblation of eternal love, because Christ had freely and eternally ordained it — the Savior dedicating Himself to death through the words: "This is my Body, which is

[116]1 Pet. 2:9.

given for you"; "This is the chalice, the New Testament in my Blood, which shall be shed for you."

The Sacrifice of the Cross, the external expression of the fixed resolve of Christ's soul, was the perfection of His oblation at the Last Supper. Like the offering in the Cenacle, it was free. His enemies outwardly inflicted upon Him physical torture, outrage, ignominy, and contempt, with absolute freedom; but they did so only because Christ offered Himself and suffered of His own free will.

The oblation in Heaven differs from the Sacrifice of the Cross and the offering in the Cenacle. Before the throne of the Father, Christ ever pleads for us with the infinite merits of His Passion and death, and all the virtues of His earthly life. On this oblation, devoid of suffering and sorrow, and in which love mounts highest, the Eternal Father gazes with satisfaction.

In the Mass, where these three offerings are mystically renewed, the virtues of Christ's life of self-extinction in all their comprehensive unity are mirrored before souls, and the Redeemer dies a bloodless death through the ministry of His earthly priests, who are to "show the death of the Lord until He comes."[117] In the mystical renewal of the celestial offering, the Mass echoes Christ's heavenly voice of continual intercession, beautifully illustrating the doctrine of the Communion of Saints, and the union of the Church Triumphant with the Church Militant and the Church Suffering. And while the haunting harmonies of Heaven blend with the soothing strains of the music of earth, man embraces and is embraced by his God.

[117] 1 Cor. 11:26.

To receive Holy Communion and to offer ourselves to Him who daily immolates Himself for us — this it is that completes and renders most efficacious for us the eucharistic oblation.

"Behold, I offered myself wholly unto my Father for thee; I gave also my whole Body and Blood for thy food, that I might be wholly thine, and that thou mightest continue mine to the end. But if thou stand upon thyself, and dost not offer thyself freely unto my will, the oblation is not complete, neither will there be entire union between us."[118]

The realization of the love that urged Christ to empty Himself for us, the conviction of what we receive who have nothing to offer to Christ but our miserable selves, will inflame our souls with a love that will consume in them whatever would offend the sacramental Savior.

The nature of our offering, if we would imitate Christ through the union of our offering with His, will correspond with the main features of His oblations in their successive forms. Like Christ's, our self-surrender will be progressive.

Christ's offering in the Cenacle was the expression of infinite, eternal love that overflowed on Calvary, for "greater love than this no man hath, that a man lay down his life for his friends."[119] Our initial act of self-oblation will also spring from a heart that beats with sincere love of God, and which, no matter the price, can rest only in Him.

This first act of self-surrender will be permanent. Self-denial will prove its sincerity. A soul so influenced by divine

---

[118] *Imitation of Christ*, Bk. 4, ch. 8.
[119] John 15:13.

love that it is seized with a great desire for God, will not, no matter how searching the test, shrink from impending trial. Cleansed and exalted by the love incident to this first act of pure devotion, it will be calm and carefree in the bitterest suffering.

The primal act of self-dedication develops, as did Christ's, when actual trial must be encountered. God searches the soul according to the quality of its love, with outward pressure and humiliation, with aridity, and with an appalling sense of abandonment. Darkness may envelop it — the want of human sympathy, an almost despairing consciousness of its own weakness, loneliness supreme, and the affrighting onslaught of temptation emphasizing its solitariness, may often chill the warmth of the love with which it made its first act of self-sacrifice. Agonizing pain, the piercing nails, the excruciating torture of the thorns, and lowering clouds carrying with them the darkness of desolation — these may almost crush the soul, and all but extinguish the light of Heaven.

But with grace triumphant in the soul, self-love dies under these trials; thoughts and feelings roaming through imagination's barren waste are banished. The soul's offering is now thoroughly chastened — more mature, more subdued. The will rules with majestic mastery.

The third act of self-surrender imitates Christ's intercession for us in Heaven. It is the ascendancy of grace in a soul that suffers with perfect resignation. This stage of self-oblation is redolent of the peace of God. It is the rededication of the soul after the storm has passed. Dominated by divine love, it has a livelier sense of the Divine Presence. During its suffering, it has gained conscious consolation and support. The angel of comfort has appeared to it in its agony.[120] Within, the soul is at rest. It is amply repaid for its struggle by the more secure possession of its God.

As they did in Christ, so these three forms of self-oblation may succeed or combine with one another in us, either partially or fully. The spirit of the Mass inspires them all, making them conducive to our spiritual development. Collectively, they are the infallible test of the highest ideal of religion, the union of the heart of the creature with the heart of Christ. We have benefited but little by the reception of the Blessed Sacrament if we do not freely forego sin and turn, body and soul, to our God — in short, if we do not experience in a common consciousness of love that we are Christ's and Christ is ours.

From this common consciousness of love must also spring the blessed hope that the eucharistic God will hereafter unite us to Himself, presenting us, in whose souls He has traced His image, to His Father, as the trophies of His Passion and death, and as the fruition of His infinite longing to be one with us.

Before we ask of Christ any fresh gift, our first and most important duty at Mass — and particularly before Holy Communion — is to offer ourselves with strong faith, absolute trust, and sincere love to Him who offers Himself for us, and who enters into us to establish the closest of all unions with our souls. Our oblation must resemble His. He is our food; we must be the food of His inconceivable desire to fashion us after Himself. While the offering of ourselves is His gift, He accepts it as our very own. This is the best recompense that our poverty

---

[120]Cf. Luke 22:43.

can make for the prodigality of the God of love. "My son, give me thy heart."[121]

We will use the time of thanksgiving most profitably, and our lives will be chains of gold studded with the daily renewals of the one mutual act of common self-surrender, if we importune the sacramental God for the grace to persevere in self-oblation, so that our sacrifice may be, like His, constant; for, says Lacordaire, "a Victim to be destroyed for sin, but a living and a dying Victim whose sacrifice was never interrupted: this is Jesus Christ."[122]

---

[121]Prov. 23:26.

[122]Henri Dominique Lacordaire (1802-1861), French Dominican preacher.

Chapter Seventeen

∞

How you can find Christ through your crosses

In assuming our nature, Christ became a sacrificial victim for the sins of the world. "God so loved the world as to give His only-begotten Son; that whosoever believeth in Him may not perish, but may have life everlasting."[123] His every act was sacrificial through His perfect obedience to the will of the Father even unto the death of the Cross.[124] But Christ's self-oblation did not end with His death. "For that He continueth forever, hath an everlasting priesthood whereby He is able also to save forever them that come to God by Him; always living to make intercession for us."[125]

In the Old Law, not the slaying of the victim, but the offering of its blood was the sacrifice. Christ's death — of which all the sacrifices of the Mosaic dispensation were but figures — was raised to a higher sphere by His ascension. "Christ, having become a high priest of the good things to come, by a greater and more perfect tabernacle not made with hand, that is, not of this creation: neither by the blood of goats, or of calves, but by His own blood, entered once into the holies, having obtained eternal redemption. For if the blood of goats and of

[123]John 3:16.
[124]Phil. 2:8.
[125]Heb. 7:24-25.

oxen, and the ashes of a heifer, being sprinkled, sanctify such as are defiled, to the cleansing of the flesh; how much more shall the blood of Christ, who, by the Holy Spirit, offered Himself unspotted unto God, cleanse our conscience from dead works, to serve the living God? And therefore, He is the mediator of the new testament: that, by means of His death, for the redemption of those transgressions, which were under the former testament, they that are called may receive the promise of eternal inheritance."[126]

In Heaven, Christ exercises the fullness of His priesthood. To Heaven the Redeemer carried the accumulated sanctity of His earthly life of unprecedented self-denial, sealed with its perfection, His death. He has "entered once into the holies," there to continue to offer Himself for us; to sustain and to perfect us children of the redeemed. Before His Father, Christ, decked with the diversified beauty of His glorified humanity, intercedes for us, and wills that we share in His propitiatory oblation, on which the earthly offering is grounded.

But the two oblations are really one, for the Priest and Victim are the same. To complete the Holy Sacrifice, the priest, not the people, must consume the Sacred Species. The one duty of the laity is union with the priest, that they may so offer the Mass as if it were their own offering, and thus share with him its grace and virtue.

Doing this, their faith will reveal to them every detail of Christ's martyrdom. The love that brought Him down from Heaven will burn in their hearts. They will marvel at His obedience to the divine will in the weariness and toil of His

[126]Heb. 9:11-15.

mission among men. They will enter the judgment hall of Pilate with Him, and hear His unjust condemnation. The heartlessly cruel betrayal by one of the chosen Twelve will loom large before them. They will behold Him crimsoned with His blood as He contends with death beneath the olives. They will see Him mocked, and scourged, and spat upon.

They will observe how eagerly He embraces the Cross, and watch Him staggering and falling under its crushing weight. They will gaze with sorrow upon Him stretched on its hard wood, every bone numbered.[127] They will listen to His prayer for His executioners in the very act of crucifixion.[128] They will look on Him, the God-Man, suspended in midair between two outcasts, with burning thirst faintly reflecting His thirst of soul for the reclamation of the sinner.[129]

They will behold all this, and then rise in spirit up to Heaven, where they will see the same divine humanity, eternally exalted and beyond the pale of pain, offered for us to the Eternal Father. Thus associated with the priest in the mystical sacrifice that unites Heaven and earth, man applies the grace of the Redemption, the efficacy of which depends on Christ's daily oblation in the Mass and His perpetual intercession in Heaven.

It is the grace of the Holy Eucharist as a sacrifice that shows very clearly the distinction between it and the other sacraments. These latter were instituted either to restore or to increase the spiritual life of the soul. Baptism, for instance, ministers only

[127] Ps. 21:17 (RSV = Ps. 22:17).
[128] Luke 23:34.
[129] John 19:28.

to our spiritual regeneration. Penance at times does likewise; and again, for the soul free from mortal sin, it serves to further its sanctification by giving it an increase of grace.

Indeed, the other sacraments exhaust their power through the communication of grace. The Holy Eucharist does more. It gives the Author of grace and comprehends the whole divine economy of salvation. It is a second Incarnation, or rather, an extension of all the benefits of Christ's taking on of our flesh. It is an act of infinite thanksgiving to God. It unites and is the pledge of the union of the members of Christ's Mystical Body. It is the divine sanction for man's salvation, because it daily renews, and applies to his soul, the merits of Christ's Passion and death.

Again, the Holy Eucharist differs from the other sacraments because it is the reason for their efficacy, inasmuch as they depend upon the merits of Christ's Death, which the Blessed Sacrament alone perpetuates. As regards its own end, the Holy Eucharist is all-embracing in its scope, influencing the entire sacramental system, since it continues the Sacrifice of the Cross, whence the other sacraments derive the effect of their manifold objects.

Once more, while the other sacraments benefit only the living, the Blessed Sacrament extends beyond time. Being the bloodless renewal of Christ's death, and the constant manifestation of His intercession in Heaven, in its pleading to the saints in glory and for the souls in Purgatory, it is universal in its application.

Thus does it unify the whole kingdom of Christ's redeeming love, uniting the children of the Church Militant with their brethren of the Church, both Triumphant and Suffering.

Like the love of Him who is daily offered in the Holy Sacrifice, the Holy Eucharist's power of adoration, propitiation, and intercession is infinite. At the Mass, the prolific stream of grace ever flows from the heart of Christ into souls purchased by His blood.

What, then, in the words of Cardinal Newman,[130] is "so piercing, so thrilling, so overcoming, as the Mass, said as it is among us?" The spirit of this greatest action that can be on earth must be ours, if we are to be conformed to our eucharistic God. Deep sorrow for sin should be ours as often as we assist at the Sacrifice that rejoices Heaven and earth, and receive Him who for us was "led as a sheep to the slaughter."[131]

What a contrast between our self-indulgence and Christ's self-denial! The Savior immolated Himself, draining the chalice of suffering to its bitterest dregs, and He continually offers Himself on the altar and in Heaven for us who are so full of self and so niggardly in His service. Only when we crucify self do we find Christ. "They that are Christ's have crucified their flesh with the vices and concupiscences."[132] Self-renunciation in the anguish of earthly loss, in the most trying humiliations, and in the pain that nails us to the Cross with Christ, will prove that the Mass has transfigured our souls by conforming them to the sacramental God.

In imitation of the sacrificial Victim of Calvary and of the Mass, who in Heaven ever pleads for us, we must, with a

---

[130]Cardinal John Henry Newman (1801-1890), English cardinal, theologian, and spiritual writer.

[131]Isa. 53:7.

[132]Gal. 5:24.

constancy that knows "no change, nor shadow of alteration,"[133] strive after the perfection of sanctity: Crucifixion with Christ. By practicing lifelong self-denial, we can be assured of realizing this holy ideal.

[133]James 1:17.

Biographical Note

∞

John A. Kane
(1883-1962)

∞

Born in Philadelphia in 1883, John Kane attended St. Mary's Seminary in Baltimore, Maryland, and St. Charles Borromeo Seminary in Overbrook, Pennsylvania, and was ordained for the Archdiocese of Philadelphia in 1912.

Known for his devotion to the Holy Eucharist, Fr. Kane was the first pastor in his archdiocese to introduce and to receive permission to hold all-night adoration of the Blessed Sacrament. He placed great importance on Catholic education of the young and succeeded in filling to overflowing his parish school of St. Madeline's in Ridley Park. In addition, he actively sought to educate adults in their Faith, and he was a pioneer in initiating a weekly religion class for them.

Fr. Kane was known during his lifetime for his great love of prayer and meditation, and his several books give proof of the wisdom gleaned from so many hours of contemplation. His writings bespeak a profound love of Christ and a warm understanding of the Catholic layman's struggle to achieve holiness. His words offer Catholics practical insight and encouragement to seek a deeper union and friendship with God.